Who doesn't marvel at the account of David's decision to spare the life of King Saul in the cave?

Who doesn't ask why David was a man after God's own heart?

But have you ever wondered what to do after you "mess up"?

Read this incredible book and you'll discover truths that just may set you free!

—THURLOW SPURR
MUSICAL DIRECTOR, TELEVISION PERSONALITY

While the story of David is not a new one, Cam's fresh approach reminds us that each of the virtues of David's life can speak to us profoundly. Anyone wanting to develop a lifestyle that is "after God's own heart" will enjoy what the Spirit of God has to say about discovering the secrets of the psalmist.

—SHAUN McCLELLAN
WORSHIP PASTOR, DENVER FIRST CHURCH

CAMERON FLORIA

DAVID'S 7 SECRETS

HIGHERLIFE
PUBLISHING & MARKETING, INC.

www.ahigherlife.com

David's 7 Secrets
What God Saw in David's Heart, What He is Looking for in
  Yours.
By Cameron Floria

Published by HigherLife Publishing and Marketing, Inc.
100 Alexandria Boulevard
Suite 9
Oviedo, Florida 32765
(407) 563-4806
www.ahigherlife.com

Cover Design: Timothy John Santana
Editor: Libbye A. Morris

ISBN: 978-1-93918-383-5

First Edition
15 16 17 18 19 — 8 7 6 5 4 3 2 1
Printed in the United States of America

THE CONTINENTALS GLOBAL FOUNDATION

"Communicating the gospel to the world in a language it understands"

In 1967, Cam Floria founded The Continental Singers, a ministry dedicated to communicating the gospel through music and the arts. For forty-four years The Continentals carried out this mission and became a model for music ministries around the world.

The Continentals Global Foundation exists to further the work started long ago by The Continentals, building on four key values they modeled so well:

Vision. Leadership. Excellence. Impact.

Partner with us in a new season of global ministry.

Order additional copies of *David's 7 Secrets*

ContinentalsGlobalFoundation.org
President—Jim Schmidt
jim@CGFtoday.com

Are you a
MUSICIAN
with a heart after God?

Do you yearn to use your musical gifts to share His love with a hurting world? **Celebrant Singers have opportunities for you!**

- Ages 18 to 80... REALLY!
- 3 and 10 week outreaches throughout the year
- Singers, Instrumentalists, Technicians, Bus Drivers and ASL Interpreters all needed.
- Call or go online TODAY!

" *CELEBRANT SINGERS take Jesus' command seriously... 'to go where His light is dim and His voice is heard small.' They minister in places often closed to more traditional missions methods. To date, they have reached millions in all 50 states and 98 countries.* **"**

For more info:
find us online at
www.**Celebrants**.org
or call (800) 321-2500

Touching the world with God's love - Since 1977!

Jon Stemkoskis
CELEBRANT SINGERS
(800) 321-2500
www.**Celebrants**.org

Want a Celebrant Singers concert in your community? Call us today!

What kind of a man would...

really love his neighbor as himself and write,
"Lord, who may live on Your holy hill? He who
does his neighbor no wrong and casts no slur on
his fellow man?"

What kind of a man would...

lead others, one or a nation, to worship the Lord
with praise on his lips and adoration in his heart
with words like, "O Lord, our Lord, how majestic
is Your name in all the earth"?

What kind of a man would...

be so filled with remorse for sin in his life that he would fall on his face, ask and plead for forgiveness, and then say, "As far as the East is from the West, so far has He removed our transgressions from us"?

What kind of a man would...

love the Lord with all his heart and all his strength, declaring, "I love You, O Lord, my strength. I will praise You, O Lord, my God with all my heart"?

What kind of a man would...

do whatever God asked him to do, and pray,
"lead me, show me, train me, direct my path to
do Your will"?

What kind of a man would...

have the moral excellence to live out the great
ancient virtues of courage, perseverance, loyalty,
honesty, justice, patience, generosity, humility,
and faith?

What kind of a man would...

announce to the world, "I am a man of prayer"?

This book is affectionately dedicated with love to all my children but especially to my two youngest sons, Ridge Cameron Floria and Radcliff Kai David Floria, who grew up with King David; so much so, we put "David" in the middle of Rad's name and of course because he is really Rad Kai, he never uses it!

My desire for all of you: Bram, Ballad, Jennifer, Barb, Ryan, Regan, Raeshell, Ridge and Rad is that you will pursue becoming people after God's heart. I know each of you wants this for your own life and your partners and your children's lives as well.

Immerse your life into Romans chapter 12 and you will be on your way.

Love, Dad

biographical thriller from beginning to end!

—Ralph Carmichael
Songwriter, Arranger

Everyone has a story. Especially David! Of all the people God could have chosen to be a hero of the faith, David certainly seems like an unlikely candidate. In the book *David's Seven Secrets*, Cam Floria has managed to mine out fresh insights from David's life story providing a beautiful catalyst to breakthroughs of the heart. In case your heart for God has grown a little calloused over the years, I suggest you pick up this great book that is likely to make your heart beat a little harder in all the right ways.

—Monty Kelso
Slingshotgroup
Next Level People. Next Level Churches.

There is King David, and there is royally flawed David. Cameron Floria has managed to take an ancient story we all know so well and glean powerful current insights from David's life lessons as though they were ripped from yesterday's headlines. *David's Seven Secrets* is a treasure of inspiration for anyone desiring to be a person after God's own heart, such as a royally flawed guy like me.

—Jim Schmidt
President, Continentals Global Foundation

The thing that makes *David's 7 Secrets* such a treasure is that it is not simply the compilation of a gifted man's excellent writing—it is the compilation of a godly man's personal journey and invitation to join him in a passionate pursuit of the heart of God! What was it that God saw in David's heart? And what is He looking for in yours? Find out in Cameron Floria's refreshing new take on a very old story!

—Bob Hallman
Senior Pastor, Crossroads Christian Fellowship
Founder/President, Kauai Bible College

Who doesn't love to read David's wonderful Psalms?

Who doesn't know the story of David and Goliath?

Who doesn't relate to the relationship of David and Jonathan?

to be one who is labeled as a man or woman after God's own heart, you will find this book a great treasure of inspiration and encouragement in your pursuit of putting God's glory on display in your life!

—Pastor Michael Mahoney
Pastor of Administration,
Grace Community Church, Sun Valley, CA

I've known Cam Floria since 1971 and his writing and insight are born from a lifetime of great victory mixed with loss and defeat, a strong faith that will not give up and a heart that beats for the kingdom of God. David, like all of us, experienced victory, loss, heartbreak, failure and the agony of disobedience but he was restored and, most of all, loved by the Heavenly Father. I hope this book will help you identify the places in your life that need to be overwhelmed by God's grace.

—Wayne Watson
Recording Artist

Cam Floria's study of David's heart will lead you to better understand two things: why David was Israel's greatest king; and how God dealt with David giving us guidance in how we, too, can be men and women after God's own heart. Not a theological treatise, this book is a practical guide to draw the Christ-follower closer to the Father in our daily lives.

—Dr. Byron Spradlin, president
Artists in Christian Testimony Intl,
Brentwood, TN

One of my favorite rooms in our home is my library. Over on one wall there are shelves holding approximately 500 books. I'm not claiming to have read them all as yet, but I'm working on it! The reason I mention this is to establish myself as a devoted reader, so that when I tell you Cam Floria's book, *David's 7 Secrets*, is a must read you will take me seriously. Cam has assembled an astounding compilation of historical facts, and there has been a lot of research involved.

Being a musician, I dearly loved his references to, and inclusion of, many of our most precious old gospel songs. But best of all, I find his continual quotations of Scripture throughout the book absolute proof that we've got the true picture of King David. This is an exciting

What does it mean to be a man of God? What does it look like? How is it expressed?

Where does one begin? Cameron Floria explores the life of David to reveal from the Scriptures seven key characteristics of the heart that not only marked his life and love and walk with God, but also marks and calls for ours as well.

—Denny Bellesi
Pastor Emeritus, Coast Hills Community Church
Author with Leesa Bellesi, *Kingdom Assignment*

Cam Floria's book is a timeless gem…a rare and precious peek into not only David's heart, but God's…a must read for every serious Christian.

—Jon Stemkoski,
Founder and President, Celebrant Singers

David was many things – saint, sinner, king, poet, musician and more. But to understand this biblical icon, we must understand what scripture means when it says that he was "a man after God's own heart." The way into that truth cannot be fully understood by didactic scholarship alone. What Cam Floria has done with his new book is to take us inside the meaning of that arresting phrase. Cam is himself a magnificent musician who opens the door into both the heart of God and the heart of David. Sharing that journey has touched my heart. I know it will do the same for all who read and listen to this masterful work.

—Norm Nelson, PhD
President and Host, Compassion Radio

I have known Cam Floria for more than 30 years and have always been moved by his love of Scripture and especially his study of the life of David. In this book, Cam captures his years of study and provides an excellent overview of the life of David and gives the reader an insightful view of what made David a man after God's own heart. Cam has captured seven practical qualities of David's life that, if applied to the life of the reader, will strengthen faith and trust in God's provision for every day. I found the book refreshing and extremely observant of those qualities that marked David's life. This book gives the motivation to persevere and strive after that which would mark any person as one who longs to be transformed in the image of Christ. If you desire

The Bible clearly says David was, "A man after God's own heart." Though he was not a perfect man, he loved God passionately and allowed the Holy Spirit to keep him close to his maker.

God loves and wants that from all of us, and Cam reveals how David learned to maintain that precious relationship. We should all imitate him to get that same incalculable result.

—PAT BOONE
RECORDING ARTIST/ACTOR

My friend Cam Floria is many things...relentless visionary, radical risk-taker, and a man after God's heart. I have known Cam for over 30 years and have seen him persevere time and again, pushing through many obstacles, to expand the Kingdom of Christ around the world through music when others would have long given up. I can see how David is a character to whom Cam relates and about whom he felt called to write. There are many similarities between them...the primary of which is a passionate unyielding desire to pursue and know the heart of God. Cam takes us not only into the externals about David, but more importantly into what drove him deep within. As I read about the life of David in these pages, I am once again brought to my knees in complete surrender to an amazing Creator, Father, and pursuer of my heart. Grab a cup of coffee, find your own "lava rock cliff" and read this book! You will be changed and—like Cam, and David—you will not be able to resist laying yourself wide open with complete abandon to knowing the heart of the Father.

—JOE HUNTSMAN, MBA, MA
FORMER CONTINENTAL DIRECTOR
CEO, SOUTHERN ORTHOCARE

David's 7 Secrets is an incredibly helpful look into David's life and how the lessons God taught him can change mine! Cameron Floria has written a solidly Biblical and historical book that is inspirational, educational, and most of all, practical. I found it difficult to put down and was encouraged and challenged by what I read. I would highly recommend "Secrets" to anyone who wants to become a man or woman after God's own heart!

—GLENN GUNDERSON
SENIOR OR LEAD PASTOR, FIRST BAPTIST, POMONA, CA

TABLE OF CONTENTS

INTRODUCTION

I FIND THAT I relate to David's life in many ways, having spent the last 25 years delving into his personality, motives, actions and yes, even his secrets. If you know his story, chances are you relate to him too. Throughout my life I have had to face many of my own giants, both in the great opportunities that God brought my way, as well as the challenges that came as a result of my own mistakes. Maybe that's why the life of David has always intrigued me so. He was a passionate worshiper of course. I can relate to that. I also relate to how the Lord continued to love and even use David despite the times he messed up. God's amazing grace for David and for me hopefully gives you hope as well.

The opportunities and struggles of my own life have resulted in their good and bad endings. Some of the good things that happened for me: winning my college conference tennis championships in the 50's, beginning the Continental Singers in the 60's, creating the Christian Artists' Seminar in the Rockies in the 70's along with the Jeremiah People, doing 1,000 live concerts in the U.S. plus hundreds more internationally in the 80's, and developing the Young Continentals in the 90's. There were also a few personal physical achievements: climbing Kilimanjaro in Africa at 19,340 feet, summiting Aconcagua in Argentina at nearly 23,000 feet, and later going to the base camps of Mt. Everest and Anapurna in Nepal.

I also had to face some serious challenges because of poor decisions regarding my own choices, which resulted in hurt, pain, and grief to my family, myself, and others: dealing with divorce and fearing I might lose my position—even in the ministries God used me to create—experiencing what it was like to have my wings broken, not just clipped, but useless, hanging to my sides, feeling just like David did in Psalm 40 and clinging to the Lord as he pulled me out of the pit. I found myself having to navigate a bankruptcy with the Continental Board of Directors in the 2000's, but then watched as the Lord brought us out on the other side with a better and stronger future ministry through the Continentals Global Foundation that is still making it possible for talented Christian youth to have the "Continental Life Changing Experience" wherever they live in the world.

So you see, I am not writing from the perspective of having it all together. My life, like David's and possibly like your own life, is filled with flaws and imperfections— amazingly none of which has disqualified me from being loved, adored, and even used by God. Living the Christian life now, though, is harder than when I was a kid or head of a ministry. The distractions of the world are so many and the persecutions coming are very real. It's the reason I wrote this book and am personally focusing hard on becoming a person after God's heart. We need to be strong and willing to stand up for what we believe. We were born for this time. Let's get ready to do our part. That's what I'm doing.

FOREWORD

MANY GREAT BOOKS have been written about King David. When I first thought about writing this book, I naively thought it might be the first one that would be focused just on David's heart.

Then one day, on a sudden impulse, I went to Google and typed in "David, a man after God's own heart." To my amazement, there were 2,900,000 entries on the subject! This was shocking information for someone about to write a book on this subject.

I could have been devastated, but in my experience, I knew God either had a plan for me to write this for myself, write it for people like you, or maybe, just to be able to talk about it, intelligently, to someone.

So my thoughts of concern quickly turned into a more excited motivation. If that many creative people have written or spoken about this subject, just think how important this must be and how many people might be interested in knowing the *secrets* of becoming a person after God's own heart?

Are you one of those people? I hope so. If so, this is for you.

Although this book does recount some of David's famous exploits and adventures, it is primarily about his heart. That's where God looked and about which He said, "The Lord does not look at the things man looks at. Man looks at the outward appearance, but the Lord looks at the heart." (1 Sam. 16:7). So the heart is where we will look, too.

The heart is where we will find *David's Seven Secrets*. What God saw in David's heart, He can also see in your heart if you are willing to embrace it, believe it, and then act on it.

❮ ❯

After many of my pastor friends read the pages to follow, each of them encouraged me to provide a Bible study to accompany this book. So I have added guidelines for a simple, easy-to-lead Bible study at the back of this book. My prayer is that it helps further your walk with God!

PRELUDE

The heart of the matter...is the heart!

"Search me, O God, and know my heart; test me and
know my anxious thoughts. See if there is any offen-
sive way in me, and lead me in the way everlasting."
—DAVID, PSALM 139:23–24

"Out of the overflow of the heart, the mouth speaks."
—JESUS, MATTHEW 12:34

Open the eyes of my heart, Lord.
Open the eyes of my heart.
I want to see you,
I want to see you.
—WORDS AND MUSIC BY PAUL BALOCHE

D AVID IS ONE of those biblical characters whose adventures and successes people love to read and hear about.
But the greatest and most compelling thing about
David is totally different than all the activity surrounding his
vibrant life. It is more important than all the battles he waged
and armies he conquered. It looms larger than all Israel's borders
he expanded and richer than the billions of dollars' worth of gold
and silver and things he accumulated.

It was a secret so amazing, so powerful, so wonderful, and yet
so awesome that God actually said, "I have found David, son of
Jesse, a man after my own heart...." (Acts 13:22) The secret was
in David's heart and only God could see it. Everyone else missed
it. The secret of what God saw is found in David's life story, his

struggles, his own writings and songs, his prayers, his worship, and his motives.

There are seven secrets. The Christian life is about these seven secrets. Now we will begin to expose each one, capture it, and make it our own! Wouldn't it be fantastic if one day God would look down at your heart and say, "There is a person after my own heart, a person who will do whatever I want him or her to do"?

> The secret of what God saw is found
> in David's life story, his struggles, his
> own writings and songs, his prayers,
> his worship, and his motives.
>
> 7 SECRETS

In Jeremiah 17:10, God says, "I, the Lord, search the heart and examine the mind to reward man according to his conduct." Here are four versions of 2 Chronicles 16:9:

- "For the eyes of the Lord range throughout the earth to strengthen those whose hearts are fully committed to him" (NIV).

- And they "run to and fro throughout the whole earth, to make Himself strong in behalf of those whose heart is blameless before Him" (TAB).

- And they "search back and forth across the whole earth, looking for people whose hearts are perfect towards Him" (TLB).

- And they "Move to and fro throughout the earth that He may strongly support those whose heart is completely His" (NAS).

All of these versions of this verse wonderfully demonstrate that God is promising to strengthen and support any person whose heart is fully committed to Him. He is looking for your committed heart right now! What does He see in your heart?

Have you ever wondered what part of you is your heart? Surely it is more than the muscle beating in your chest. Is it your mind, what you think, what you dream, and what motivates you? Is it your spirit, that part of you that makes up your personality and emotions? Is it your soul, that part of you that is life itself and what we think of as God's, eternally? Which one is He looking at to see if you are committed enough to Him to be a person after His heart?

When the Bible talks about the heart, it is talking about all of these inner parts at the same time, all of who you are on the inside. This is your heart. This is the committed part of you He is looking for. His eyes sweep throughout the earth looking for your committed heart. This is absolutely breathtaking!

Consider these final and powerful words David said to his son, Solomon, as he neared the end of his life, knowing that Solomon was to carry on his legacy: "And you, my son Solomon, acknowledge the God of your father, and serve Him with wholehearted devotion and with a willing mind, for the Lord searches every heart and understands every motive behind the thoughts. If you seek Him, He will be found by you… Consider now, for the Lord has chosen you"! (1 Chron. 28:9–10). God chose David, and Jesus said the same of his followers, including you and me. "You did not choose Me, but I chose you and appointed you to go and bear fruit" (John 15:16). That is such an incredible truth. So now, what about bearing fruit and becoming a person after God's heart?

> When the Bible talks about the heart, it is talking about all of these inner parts at the same time, all of who you are on the inside.

7 S E C R E T S

Does it motivate you, knowing that you have been chosen by the Lord to go and bear fruit? How does it make you feel to know He is looking at your heart today to see if you are committed to Him?

What did God see in David's heart, deep down, that made him the Lord's special choice? These are the secrets that will unfold, one by one, from his own life and his own words. He faced his giants and did what God wanted him to do.

One

BRING ON THE GIANTS

DAVID'S SECRET #1
He Did What God Wanted Him to Do

"I HAVE FOUND DAVID, son of Jesse, a man after my own heart; He will do everything I want him to do" (God, Acts 13:22).

"Show me the way I should go, for to You, I lift up my soul. Teach me to do Your will, for You are my God; may Your good spirit lead me on level ground...for I am Your servant" (David, Ps. 143:8, 10, 12).

I am a servant, I am listening for my name,
I sit here waiting, I've been looking at the game
That I've been playing, and I've been staying much the same.
When you are lonely, you're the only one to blame.

I am a servant, I am waiting for the call,
I've been unfaithful, so I sit here in the hall.
How can you use me when I've never given all,
How can you choose me when you know I'd quickly fall.

So you feed my soul and you make me grow,
And you let me know you love me.
And I'm worthless now, but I've made a vow,
I will humbly bow before thee.
O please use me, I am lonely.

I am a servant getting ready for my part,

There's been a change, a rearrangement in my heart.

At last I'm learning, there's no returning once I start.

To live's a privilege, to love is such an art.

But I need your help to start,

O, please purify my heart. I am your servant.

—"I AM A SERVANT," WORDS AND MUSIC

BY LARRY NORMAN

In the days before kings, prophets ruled as judges in the land. The last of these great prophets was Samuel. When he was old, he appointed his two sons as judges, but they turned away from God and chose dishonest gain and accepted bribes and perverted justice.

So the elders of Israel came to Samuel and asked for a king to rule over them like all the other nations had. Samuel was displeased with their request, so he prayed to the Lord.

The Lord told him, "Listen to all that the people are saying to you; it is not you they have rejected, but they have rejected me as their King… Warn them solemnly and let them know what the king who will reign over them will do." (1 Sam. 8:7, 9)

Samuel followed God's instructions and brought together members of each of the tribes of Israel. Benjamin was selected. From Benjamin, clan by clan, Matri was chosen, and from his clan the family of Kish was chosen. From Kish, his son Saul was chosen. His description was like this: "An impressive young man without equal among the Israelites, a head taller than any of the others" (1 Sam. 9:2).

Samuel said to all the people, "Do you see the man the Lord has chosen? There is no one like him among all the people" (1 Sam. 10:24).

Samuel followed God's instructions
and brought together members
of each of the tribes of Israel.

7 SECRETS

Saul had a great beginning. He was thirty when he became the king and immediately put an army together. The battles with the Philistines began, and Israel's army inflicted punishment on all the other neighboring kingdoms as well. However, over the course of his reign, Saul became less dependent on the Lord and more confident of his own abilities and successes. His instructions from the Lord, through Samuel, were only partially fulfilled. Once, in an impatient moment, he offered up a burnt offering, something only the prophets or priests were allowed to do.

Then came Samuel's devastating words: "You acted foolishly. You have not kept the command the Lord your God gave you; if you had, he would have established your kingdom over Israel for all time. But now, your kingdom will not endure; the Lord has sought out *a man after his own heart* and appointed him leader of his people..." (emphasis mine, 1 Sam. 13:13–14).

Soon word came to Samuel from the Lord: "Fill your horn with oil, and be on your way. I am sending you to Jesse of Bethlehem. I have chosen one of his sons to be king" (1 Sam. 16:10).

JESSE'S YOUNGEST SON

A big change was in the wind for Israel, though it would not happen for some time. In the beginning, Samuel was afraid to anoint one of Jesse's sons for fear that Saul would have him killed. So the Lord told him to take a heifer with him and say he had come to sacrifice it to the Lord. He was to invite Jesse and his sons to the occasion.

When they arrived, Samuel saw the eldest son, Eliab, who was strong and tall. He thought for sure this was the one the Lord had selected. But the Lord said these immortal words: "Do not consider his appearance or his height, for I have rejected him. The Lord does not look at the things man looks at. Man looks at the outward appearance, but *the Lord looks at the heart*" (emphasis mine, 1 Sam. 16:7).

One by one, seven of Jesse's sons were paraded before Samuel, and none was selected. Because none of them were chosen, Samuel asked Jesse if those were all of his sons. Jesse replied that the youngest son was not there; he was tending the sheep. Samuel told Jesse to send for him immediately and that he would not sit down until he arrived.

When the youngest son arrived, Samuel saw a boy with a fine appearance and handsome features, ruddy from being out with the sheep day and night.

Then the Lord said, "Rise and anoint him; he is the one" (1 Sam. 16:12). Samuel anointed him in the presence of his family, and from that day on, the spirit of the Lord came on David in power.

What an amazing beginning for a young teenager! You can imagine all the things that might have been going through his mind. For sure, it was the experience of a lifetime, his destiny laid out before him, never to be forgotten. Nothing but a kid watching some sheep one moment, in line to be the future king the next.

The teen years are the time when a young person needs to make the choice to become someone whose heart is fully committed to the Lord. Giants are just ahead, and it's time to get prepared. God's Word is the armor that's necessary, along with an unwavering desire to become all that God wants him or her to be. And isn't it just like the Lord to choose the least likely and weakest to become the greatest?

"Weak" was not a description for David from that point on, however, as the Spirit of God came on him in power. He was courageous enough to chase down a lion at one time and a bear another, while rescuing a helpless little lamb. Without a spear or a club, he was able to kill each predator with his bare hands, as he would relate to King Saul at a future time.

But for now, David went back to the sheep with his sling, his harp, his songs, and his thoughts. He could see God's greatness in those hills and skies of Bethlehem. Without a doubt, he reaffirmed his loyalty and devotion to the God who was laying out the plan, the call, and the destiny for the rest of his life.

In time, he earned the reputation as being one who sang and played the harp beautifully. So when Saul began suffering spells of deep depression, panic, paranoia, and anxiety, along with evil hallucinations of all kinds, the young shepherd from Bethlehem was asked to come to play and sing to soothe the king's crazed moods. The music calmed his spirit.

> Without a doubt, he reaffirmed his loyalty and devotion to the God who was laying out the plan, the call, and the destiny for the rest of his life.

7 SECRETS

David went back and forth from his father's ranch to the palace to play for the emotionally disturbed King Saul. These occasional visits eventually culminated in a confrontation with a giant!

What about giants in your life and mine? Are we strong enough to follow through with what we know God wants us to do, even if a giant stands in the way? Like the apostle Paul said a thousand years after David killed Goliath, "If God is for us, who can be against us?" (Rom. 8:31). Certainly not a meager giant!

We all have to identify our own giants and be sure the Lord is giving us the go-ahead to stand up to them.

THE BRAZILIAN CONTINENTALS

So it was with some Brazilian Continentals who made the decision to stand up to their giants, and then actually got help from some giants as well.

Vilar Goncalves, a young man from Belo Horizonte, believed God wanted him to bring a musical program to the main auditorium in his city. The city officials did not want him to use their auditorium for a Christian concert. It was well known that the facility was used for anything but Christian activities. He was denied again and again. He persisted, though, and eventually, by paying a large rental price, he was given permission for his performance, the first ever by the Brazilian Continentals.

Following Joshua's battle plan for success, Vilar and his group went down to the auditorium the week of their premiere and marched around it every night for six nights in a row, singing, praising God, and praying that He would give them His blessing and spiritual success for their upcoming performance.

On the seventh night, after marching, they were sitting in a circle outside the auditorium, again praying, when the audience from another performance came out of the venue. The young people were ridiculed, spat upon, kicked, and derided for their beliefs. Fearing a physical attack by one of the men in the street, Vilar stood up and faced him. Vilar is an athletic, soccer-playing, well-built man, but he had no intention of violence. As he stood there, two of the men fell back, screaming, "Don't let them hurt us!" and ran off.

> What about giants in your life and mine?
> Are we strong enough to follow through
> with what we know God wants us to
> do, even if a giant stands in the way?

7 SECRETS

Suddenly, standing behind the group there appeared two men taller than nine feet, with drawn swords, looking very much like giants. The defenders appeared just in time to protect the group of young Christian Brazilians who had made the decision to face their giants and take advantage of the opportunity the Lord had opened up for them.

Throughout David's life, above all else, he wanted to do what God wanted him to do. He followed God's will and all His directions, and his mind was geared to accomplish all that God required of him. Even as a young man he wrote the following:

+ "Show me Your ways, O Lord, Teach me Your paths; guide me in Your truth and teach me, for You are God, my Savior, and my hope is in You all day long" (Ps. 25:4–5).

+ "I desire to do Your will, O my God; Your law is within my heart" (Ps. 40:8).

+ "I have set the Lord always before me" (Ps. 16:8).

God responded to him in Psalm 32:8, "I will instruct you and teach you in the way you should go; I will counsel you and watch over you."

In David's own inimitable way, to be sure that he didn't have to go it alone, he reminded the Lord, "Since You are my rock and my fortress, for the sake of Your Name, lead and guide me" (Ps. 31:3).

As a leader, David always inquired of the Lord before any military campaigns, and when he received the answer, he immediately acted on it. Someone once said, "Do not ask the Lord to guide your footsteps unless you are willing to move your feet."

Many scriptures talk about doing God's will, but 1 Thessalonians 5:16–18 speaks directly of God's will for all of us: "Be joyful always; pray continually; give thanks in all circumstances, for this is God's will for you in Christ Jesus."

In his book *The Time of Saul's Tyranny*, W. Phillip Keller wrote, "God's chief criterion for selecting special servants for mighty purposes is 'Are you willing to do My will?' This is the acid test. Despite all of an individual's other failings, if, above all else, his one consuming desire is to be 'A Man After God's Own Heart,' then he will be lifted above the turmoil of his times in great honor."

Such was David. His mature words from Psalm 139 reflect his total surrender to God's plan and will for his life: "O Lord, You have searched me, and You know me. You know when I sit and when I rise; You perceive my thoughts from afar. You discern my going out and my lying down; You are familiar with all my ways. Before a word is on my tongue, You know it completely, O Lord. You hem me in, behind and before; You have laid Your hand upon me. Such knowledge is too wonderful for me, too lofty for me to attain. Where can I go from Your Spirit? Where can I flee from Your presence? If I go up to the heavens, You are there. If I make my bed in the depths, You are there. If I rise on the wings of the dawn, if I settle on the far side of the sea, even there Your hand will guide me, your right hand will hold me fast."

Understanding that God's hand is there to hold you up as you follow His lead, how are you dealing with the giants you are coming face to face with in your life?

In addition to David's willingness to do everything God asked him to do, He had an immense integrity before men. He had a seat at God's Round Table.

Two

SIT AT GOD'S ROUND TABLE

DAVID'S SECRET #2

He Was a Man of Integrity and Virtue

JUDGE ME, O Lord, according to my righteousness, according to my integrity, oh Most High" (David, Ps. 7:8).

"David reigned over all Israel, doing what was just and right for all his people" (2 Sam. 8:15).

Since the fall of man in Genesis, there has been the choice of right and wrong. On the side of right, man developed a code of ethics down through the ages called "virtues." These were positive traits that would allow him to live peacefully and honorably and even lend a hand to his neighbors. When these standards were abused, anger, unhappiness, feelings of being wronged, and even war were often the result.

Two great Greek philosophers, Aristotle and Plato, were the first to write about and create a list of virtues. They called their list the "cardinal virtues," which were temperance, prudence, justice, and courage.

Three more virtues—faith, hope, and love, known as the "theological virtues" from the writings of the apostle Paul—were added to the "cardinal virtues" list and were adopted by the Catholic Church. These became known as the "seven cardinal virtues."

> Two great Greek philosophers, Aristotle
> and Plato, were the first to write
> about and create a list of virtues.

7 SECRETS

Good men have always strived to live by these virtues, but at the same time, there has always been the struggle with what was called "the seven deadly sins."

Around 400 AD, a Christian governor named Aurelius listed seven "heavenly virtues" to counteract "the seven deadly sins." Here is his list of virtues, along with the accompanying vice that the virtue counteracts: chastity (*lust*), temperance (*gluttony*), charity (*greed*), diligence (*sloth*), patience (*wrath*), kindness (*envy*), and humility (*pride*).

When we think of the Age of Chivalry and the romantic, shining knights of King Arthur's Round Table, we envision maidens being rescued, men of honor sitting astride horses with long jousting spears in their hands, and great battles for right. These knights also lived by a code of virtues that were carried on long after the knights had disappeared. They were courage, justice, mercy, honor, generosity, faith, nobility, and hope.

More recently, *The Book of Virtues*, which William J. Bennett wrote in 1993, contains more than eight hundred pages of poems, essays, short stories, and ancient, well-known tales in ten chapters. Bennet wrote this book to help children, their parents, and teachers understand values and virtues and their importance. The ten virtues he listed were made into a wonderful video series by public television and are named self-discipline, compassion, responsibility, friendship, work, courage, perseverance, honesty, loyalty, and faith.

So now we have the seven cardinal virtues, the heavenly virtues, the knightly virtues, and the Bennett book of virtues.

Yet just over three thousand years ago, God looked into a young man's heart, and there He found virtues that would turn that boy into the greatest and most influential leader of any age in Israel's history. He had values and virtues that would lead his lineage to Jesus Christ Himself.

So now we have the seven cardinal virtues, the heavenly virtues, the knightly virtues, and the Bennett book of virtues.

7 SECRETS

DAVID'S VIRTUES

Ten virtues are found in David's writings and in his life story, which describe his feelings and actions in all kinds of situations. They are courage, justice, loyalty, honesty, humility, perseverance, patience, faith, trust, and generosity. Let's take a closer look at each one.

COURAGE

"I've got confidence

God is gonna see me through.

No matter what the case may be, I know He's gonna fix it for me."

—"I'VE GOT CONFIDENCE," WORDS AND MUSIC BY
ANDREA CROUTCH

Ten virtues are found in David's writings
and in his life story, which describe his
feelings and actions in all kinds of situations.

7 SECRETS

Let's start with Goliath! Of all the stories of courage we can find, none has captured the imagination of young and old like David and Goliath.

The giant was more than nine and a half feet tall (three meters and a span). His armor weighed 125 pounds, and his large spear had an iron head that weighed 15 pounds. He had armor on his legs as well, and he had a shield bearer that went ahead of him. His voice rang out through the valley every morning with a challenge to anyone in the Israeli army to come fight to the death. No one ever accepted. Saul and all his army were terrified.

Saul was the tallest and most experienced warrior in his army. He was expected to fight Goliath. His son, Jonathan, an experienced fighter, who had single-handedly killed more than twenty Philistines at one time, would not go, either. So Saul offered great reward to the man who would have enough courage to stand up to this giant.

David, who was nineteen or twenty years old at this time, was bringing supplies to his brothers. He had been going back and forth from serving Saul to his father's ranch when he heard the giant's challenge. While the men of Israel ran in fear, David incredulously blurted out, "Who is this uncircumcised Philistine that he should defy the armies of the living God?" (1 Sam. 17:26).

These words echoed to the attention of the king. Once he heard David's recounting of how he had killed the lion and the bear with just his bare hands, he made the decision: let this shepherd boy, a warrior in the making, go out and stand for Israel and fight the giant.

He tried to dress David in his own tunic, armor, helmet, and sword. This would have meant that David had a full-grown stature. But as David was walking around in them, he said to Saul, "I cannot go in these because I am not used to them" (1 Sam. 17:39).

David wrote, "It is God who arms me with strength and makes my way perfect. He makes my feet like the feet of a deer..." (Ps. 18:32–33).

So, without wearing any kind of protection, he took his shepherd's staff and his sling and walked into the valley. He picked up five rounded, smooth, good-sized stones from the creek bed and walked toward Goliath.

Goliath looked David over, and he despised him. He said, "Am I a dog that you come at me with sticks?" And the Philistine cursed David by his gods. "Come here," he said, "and I will give your flesh to the birds of the air and the beasts of the field."

David said to the Philistine, "You come against me with sword, and spear, and javelin, but I come against you in the name of the Lord Almighty, the God of the armies of Israel, whom you have defied. This day the Lord will hand you over to me, and I'll strike you down and cut off your head, and the whole world will know that there is a God in Israel" (1 Sam. 17:43–46).

With that, David ran toward Goliath. Reaching into his bag, he pulled out a stone, placed it in his sling, and slung it with such power and accuracy that it sank into the giant's forehead. Goliath fell face-down on the ground before he even got close enough to swing his sword.

David ran and stood over the Philistine, drawing his sword out of the scabbard, and cut off his head, as he had told him he would do.

This episode changed David's life forever. No longer was he just a minstrel for the king. Now he was an honored hero, a hero who always gave God the credit for his victories. This time, in celebration, he wrote, "O Lord, our Lord, how majestic is Your name in all the earth" (Ps. 8:1).

A Songwriter's Challenge

Three thousand years later, Christian recording artist Michael W. Smith also wrote, "How Majestic Is Your Name." Although he didn't write it after killing a giant, Michael says it was one of his earliest songs, one he wrote even before he had recorded his first album, *The Michael W. Smith Project.*

For his entire life, Michael has been intrigued by the Psalms, so he went to a musician, David, for some insight. As he read Psalm 8, it was like the music just came out of him. It took one minute, and all of a sudden, he was singing, "How majestic is your name in all the earth." Michael said it was as if "Classical Smitty met the Doobie Brothers, given the chords in the chorus."

Like so many great musicians and artists, Michael and his wife, Debbie, started out writing for their church, Belmont Church in Nashville. Don Finto, their pastor and friend, also became Michael's mentor, in the early '80s. His new publisher at Meadowgreen suggested that he send this song to Sandi Patty. Even though he had never met her, he found a way to get a copy of it to her. She loved it, recorded it, and the rest is history.

Michael now says laughingly, "It's in eighteen different hymn books and I'm one of the few composers in there without a deceased date."

After David had killed Goliath, Saul sent him to be a commander over some of his men. Whatever Saul sent him to do, David did it so successfully that Saul gave him a high ranking in the army. But these successes also brought jealousy from Saul and warnings from his advisors that David was out for the throne.

This eventually put an end to David's career in the army. Even though he was married to Saul's daughter, the king sent messengers to his house to kill him. For many years, David was on the run, escaping the various armies that Saul kept sending out to capture him. David's bravery and courage were recounted many times during those years, but he did not give up or capitulate.

Winston Churchill once said, "Success is not final, failure is not fatal; it is courage to continue that counts." The big question is, do we have the courage to face the giants in our lives?

A Mentor's Courage

My friend and early mentor, Thurlow Spurr, has courage. I don't know anyone who has had more successes and at the same time more interrupted possibilities than Thurlow. One he loves to talk about happened in 1996, called "Jerusalem Three Thousand."

He chartered a 747 to take some singers to Israel to direct a premiere of the musical I had just finished writing for this event. It was called *David, a Man After God's Own Heart*. I'm sure we all know people who go around chartering these monster airplanes for their musical tours! *Not!*

We were part of an organization whose goal was to celebrate the three thousandth birthday of Jerusalem, and we wanted to take three thousand people to David's former capitol that summer. Most of us bought round-trip tickets, but Thurlow chartered the whole airplane. And he filled it up!

Then came disaster. Prime Minister Yitzhak Rabin was assassinated on November 4, 1995, causing huge fear and unrest in the Middle East. The people on Thurlow's 747 canceled faster than they had signed up. He was still personally liable for the $1 million cost of chartering the 747 and was now faced with an empty airplane.

Time went by, and soon things in Israel got back to normal. Undaunted, Thurlow and his staff went back to work recruiting once again. He more than filled the plane *a second time!*

The end of the story is a big success. Seven hundred singers from all over the United States and four international orchestras with more than 105 instrumentalists and eight dancers and mimes from Jerusalem and Kansas joined forces for the world premiere at the famous outdoor arena called "The David Citadel" in the corner of the western wall of Jerusalem. Thurlow conducted the music before a full audience. I felt the presence of the angels sitting around the top of the wall, and I prayed that if at all possible, God would let David himself see this musical portrayal of his life story. It was a performance and experience none of us will ever match—or forget! From the research that began for that musical in the early '90s comes the book you are reading today.

> I felt the presence of the angels sitting around the top of the wall, and I prayed that if at all possible, God would let David himself see this musical portrayal of his life story.

7 SECRETS

JUSTICE

"Right is right, even if everyone is against it; and wrong is wrong, even if everyone is for it."

—WILLIAM PENN

This was David's way. He wrote the following:

- "I will sing of Your love and justice…" (Ps. 101:1).

- "The Lord is known by His justice…" (Ps. 9:16).

- "For the Lord loves the just…" (Ps. 37:28).

David understood the principle of justice, even if a situation seemed to demand the opposite and friends were encouraging him to act on it. But the right action for justice, in David's heart, always won out.

On one occasion, when he was on the run from King Saul and living in caves, Saul actually went into the cave where David and his men were hiding. His men told David that the Lord had delivered Saul into their hands, and it was a good time to rid themselves of this king. But, as much as David wanted to be free of Saul, he acted in a different way. He said, "The Lord forbid that I should do such a thing to my master, the Lord's anointed, or lay my hand on him; for he is the anointed of the Lord" (1 Sam. 24:6). Then he said, "The Lord himself will strike him, or his time will come and he will die, or he will go into battle and perish" (1 Sam. 26:10). Then, to make a point to Saul, he crept up and cut a corner off the robe the king had laid aside.

Once Saul had left the cave, David walked to the entrance and yelled to the king with the corner of the robe in his hand, "I will not lift my hand against my master because he is the Lord's anointed! See, my father, look at this piece of your robe in my hand. I have not wronged you, but you are hunting me down to take my life. May the Lord judge between you and me, and may the Lord avenge the wrongs you have done to me, but my hand will not touch you" (1 Sam. 24:12).

Saul's response was remorseful: "Is that your voice, David, my son? And he wept aloud. You are more righteous than I....I know that you will surely be king, and the kingdom of Israel will be establish

ed in your hands." Then he pledged to stop hunting David, but in the end, was unable to keep his word (1 Sam. 16, 20).

Some years later, a civil war was fought between Judah and Israel, when David was king in Judah, and Ishbosheth, Saul's son, was the king of Israel. Two men, thinking they would be rewarded, broke into Ishbosheth's bedroom and killed him while he slept, then took his head to David. Once in David's presence, they justly faced the death penalty rather than a reward for killing the king.

LOYALTY

Loyalty is important to everyone but essential to leaders who desire a loyal staff, loyal followers, and loyal employees. We all need loyal friends and family. The armed forces demand loyalty—both to country and to comrades. Businesspeople even talk about loyalty to their particular brand. We just want those around us to be faithful friends.

God demanded loyalty when He said to Israel in the beginning, "You are to have no other gods before me." David certainly lived by a code of loyalty to his men, and he expected it in return from them. Yet this powerful virtue is seldom mentioned by name in the Bible, and only the Bennett list includes it. The heavenly virtues list it under kindness, and the cardinal virtues and knightly virtues list loyalty under "faith." God's Word talks about loyalty as faithfulness. We know that faithfulness is one of the great fruits of the Spirit listed in Galatians, chapter 5.

> Loyalty is important to everyone but essential to leaders who desire a loyal staff, loyal followers, and loyal employees.

7 SECRETS

David wrote in Psalm 18:25 and 2 Samuel 22:26, "To the faithful, you show yourself faithful." Psalm 25:10 says, "All the ways of the Lord are loving and faithful." And in Psalm 31:23, it says, "Love the Lord, all His saints, the Lord preserves the faithful...." He wrote in Psalm 37:28, "For the Lord loves the just and will not forsake his faithful ones...."

In David's Psalm 145, he wrote line after line of many of the great virtues God looks for in our hearts. I love verse 13: "The Lord is faithful to all His promises and loving toward all He has made." He expects us to also be faithful to our promises, faithful to Him, and faithful to the end.

Jesus said the words that echo in our Christian brains most days of our lives. Wouldn't you love to hear His words someday when He looks straight in your eyes and says, "Well done, good and faithful servant!" (Matt. 25:23).

I doubt if you will ever have to lay down your life because of your loyalty and faithfulness to your beliefs in God and Jesus Christ. However, in today's world, hundreds of Christians are being beheaded by extremist Muslims, and thousands of others are being killed for their faith in Arab communities in the Middle East, Africa, Afghanistan, and Pakistan, including countries like Indonesia, China, and many other places. Becoming a martyr in the twenty-first century is a real threat and possibility.

In your lifetime and mine, with animosities from our own government and outspoken critics of the Christian lifestyle here in the States, it could eventually be anyone, even a family member, who despises your commitment to the Lord.

Have you ever thought how it would be to face an enemy of your faith who asked you to deny your Christianity or die, or who just wanted to take your life because they knew you were a Christian, like some students in Kenya and Oregon who were shot because they were Christians?

> Becoming a martyr in the twenty-first
> century is a real threat and possibility.
>
> **7** S E C R E T S

Revelation 2:10 talks about persecutions that will happen
near the end of the age. Jesus said, "Be faithful, even to the point
of death, and I will give you the crown of life." Here is what He
said about it in Matthew 10:32, which deals with the loyalty He
expects from us: "Whoever acknowledges Me before men, I will
also acknowledge before my Father in heaven. But whoever dis-
owns Me before men, I will disown him before my Father in
heaven."

God looked into David's heart and found a young man who
would be loyal, faithful, and true to the very end.

HONESTY

It is clear that when God looks into your heart, and mine, He is
looking for honesty and truthfulness in all of our dealings. That
means in business, school, with friends and neighbors, at tax
time, at the mall, at the grocery store...and you can continue
this list.

David said it many times, in many different ways: "Test me,
O Lord, and try me, examine my heart and my mind; for Your
love is ever before me, and I walk continually in Your truth" (Ps.
26:2–3).

> It is clear that when God looks into your
> heart, and mine, He is looking for honesty
> and truthfulness in all of our dealings.
>
> **7** S E C R E T S

Psalm 51:6 says, "Surely you desire truth in the inner parts."

Mother Teresa said, "If you are honest, people may cheat you. Be honest anyway. For you see, in the end, it is between you and God. It was never between you and them anyway."

> "Whoever is careless with the truth in small matters cannot be trusted with important matters."
>
> —ALBERT EINSTEIN

Way back in grade school, we heard about George Washington and the cherry tree incident. In M. L. Weim's story lesson, we learned that telling the truth is a thousand times better than telling a lie. The boy's father declared to little George, after he had confessed to cutting the tree down with his little hatchet, "My son, that you should not be afraid to tell the truth is more to me than a thousand trees."

David, in his later years, wrote, "No one who practices deceit will dwell in my house; no one who speaks falsely will stand in my presence" (Ps. 101:7).

God looks at our hearts like He did David's. He is expecting you and me to live an example of honesty. Gandhi once said, "To believe in something and not live it is dishonest." That means being sincere, truthful, trustworthy, honorable, and genuine, and then living it all the time. If we do that, which means putting the Lord in the center of our lives every day, then we will also have to be living another of David's virtues: humility.

HUMILITY

> "Humble yourself in the sight of the Lord,
> Humble yourself in the sight of the Lord,
> And He will lift you up.

And He, will lift you up!"

—"HUMBLE YOURSELF,"
SONGWRITER UNKNOWN, JAMES 4:10

Although David did not write much about humility and its opposite, pride, he did live it. Every battle of any kind he ever fought, he first asked for God's help and direction. When it was over, he immediately praised and glorified God for the victory, beginning with Goliath. He knew he was anointed to be king, but there was always a humility that bled through his words and actions, even when he was faced with his own sin.

After David slayed Goliath, King Saul wanted to give David his eldest daughter in marriage. It was part of the reward, but David's attitude was, "Who am I, and what is my family...that I should become the king's son-in-law? I am only a poor man and little known." Of course, we know now that his last statement was quite short-lived! (1 Sam. 18:18, 23)

David's son, Solomon, had a lot to say about humility in his proverbs:

+ "Humility comes before honor" (Prov. 15:33).

+ "When pride comes, then comes disgrace, but with humility comes wisdom" (Prov. 11:2).

And the one we have heard our whole lives: "Pride goes before destruction, a haughty spirit before a fall" (Prov. 16:18).

Jesus left us His own words on the subject, speaking to his disciples He said, "The greatest among you will be your servant. For whoever exalts himself will be humbled, and whoever humbles himself will be exalted" (Matt. 23:11–12).

At the end of his life, after reigning as king for forty years, David spoke his last words: "When one rules over men in righteousness, when he rules in the fear of God, he is like the light of morning at sunrise on a cloudless morning, like the brightness after rain that brings grass from the earth" (2 Sam. 23:3–4). And David said of the Lord, "You save the humble, but Your eyes are on the haughty to bring them low" (2 Sam. 22:28).

David had a humble beginning as a shepherd boy. He was the youngest and the least in his family. He was the last one they thought of when the great prophet came to anoint a future king. But God looked into David's heart and saw someone He could exalt, a young man who would write, and sing, and exalt Him right back.

From that time on, David knew that someday he really would become the king. The timing was in God's hands, and in the meantime, David had to exercise another of his virtues: patience.

PATIENCE

Imagine being anointed as a future king by the great prophet in your teenage years, during a time when a prophet was never wrong, as he delivered the word of God, directly from God!

David knew from that day on that it would happen, but he didn't know all the other experiences God was going to take him through and all the things He had to first learn. It was truly an incredible journey.

The first life-changer was heading from the shepherd's field to Saul's court to play the harp and sing to soothe Saul's imbalanced, crazy moments. He was selected not only for his musical ability but was also described by Saul's attendants as being a brave man, a warrior who spoke well, was fine looking, and the Lord was with him.

Saul liked him very much and even made him one of his armor bearers. So back and forth he went, sheep to Saul, Saul to sheep, for the next five to six years. You get the feeling that he was more often in the Bethlehem hills than at Saul's court. His confrontation with Goliath happened at some point during the end of this time.

That changed everything! Some months of court intrigue and rumor followed. He succeeded in every military campaign Saul gave him. But soon, David's national popularity was more than the king or the king's attendants could handle.

David did continue to play the harp and sing for the King occasionally, but Saul refused to let him return to his father's sheep ranch. On two occasions, while David was playing, Saul was so paranoid that David had become the enemy, he tried to pin him to the wall with his spear. David fled for his life, left everything behind, and went to Samuel. He needed some support and direction.

> But soon, David's national popularity was more than the king or the king's attendants could handle.

7 SECRETS

As mentioned earlier, some amazing experiences followed. He lived as a vagabond in his own country, hiding in caves and rocky fortresses, often without food and water, outwitting Saul, who was always on the hunt for him. He had to hide in cities that turned him in to the king, feigned insanity, and was under house arrest in the Philistine city of Gath. Yet during this time, other men who were also on the run from the king came to David.

Over the next seven years, he built a sizeable guerilla army of six hundred loyal, fighting men, later known as David's Mighty Men. Many of them stayed with him the rest of his life as his bodyguards.

With these men, he plundered towns and villages of the Philistines and other enemy nations and protected Israeli ranchers from other raiding bands. And then, when David was thirty years old, Saul and his sons were killed on Mt. Gilboa, and David was anointed King of Judah in Hebron.

David exemplified patience with a deep trust in the Lord's calling on his life, and this confidence surely kept him going. God's timing is seldom man's, but God's timing is always the best.

David wrote, "I waited patiently for the Lord; He turned to me and heard my cry. He lifted me out of the slimy pit.... He set my feet on a rock and gave me a firm place to stand" (Ps. 40:1–2).

Psalm 37:7 says, "Be still before the Lord and wait patiently for Him...." And Psalm 27:14 says, "Wait for the Lord; be strong and take heart, and wait for the Lord."

> God's timing is seldom man's, but
> God's timing is always the best.

7 SECRETS

Patience can mean hanging in there during difficult and "molasses-like" progress, but persevering in the face of these unending delays and of unforeseen and often dangerous circumstances, is a different matter. That was certainly the case for David.

PERSEVERANCE

Standing strong, pushing through, not wavering, staying focused, taking the hits, continuing on through impossibilities, bearing down, taking one more step and then another, willing it, wanting it, never giving up, being determined, being driven—that is perseverance. It is also getting to the summit of Mt. Everest, where even the strongest and most experienced climbers in the world understand that once they climb into the "death zone" after

26,500 feet, only mental determination and perseverance will get them to the summit and back again.

The apostle Paul called it "pressing on." David called it "being strong, enduring, having zeal, watching, waiting and staying steadfast." In Psalm 51:10, he said, "Renew a steadfast spirit within me."

Years ago, before he became a major Christian recording artist, Wayne Watson toured with the Continental Singers. He received such overwhelming response to his solos that he believed God was calling him to dedicate his life to sharing the Gospel with his voice and his music.

After touring that summer, Wayne went back to his home-town in Louisiana with great anticipation of God catapulting him into a major career and record contract.

Nothing happened.

It was just like before. He began to doubt if he had a calling at all. Frustrated, he called me with just one question: "What more can I do to have a significant ministry as a Christian artist?"

I asked him what he was doing right then. He answered, "The same things I did before—going on tour, singing in churches around my area, in places that know me, as well as making appearances at senior-citizen complexes and even the local prison."

All I could think to say was, "Well, Wayne, just keep on doing what you are doing now. There is a spiritual principle that we find in the Bible. It says that those who are faithful in small things are liable to be given bigger things." Then I realized an even bigger principle and voiced it: "If God is in it, it can't be stopped! If He isn't, it won't happen anyway, and He has some-thing else for you to do."

Wayne persevered and kept on with the small opportunities that came his way. Soon after our discussion, he found a song called "The Touch of the Master's Hand." He immediately put it into his repertoire, and the rest is history. Word Records signed him to his first recording contract, and his international career was on its way. He found himself making a major impact on the world with his songs and his music.

Believing in God's calling on your life, coupled with perseverance to follow His direction no matter what, is an important step in being a person after God's heart. And remember, if God is in it, whatever the big dream He has given you, it cannot be stopped.

Many of the most successful people in the world faced impossible situations and found a way to keep going. Here is what some of them have said.

> Believing in God's calling on your life, coupled with perseverance to follow His direction no matter what, is an important step in being a person after God's heart.

7 SECRETS

"Most of the important things in the world have been accomplished by people who have kept on trying when there seemed to be no hope at all."

—DALE CARNEGIE

"It always seems impossible until it's done."

—NELSON MANDELA

"Every strike brings me closer to the next home run."

—BABE RUTH

"Courage and perseverance have a magical talisman
before which difficulties and obstacles vanish into thin
air."

—JOHN QUINCY ADAMS

For many long, hard, and hurtful years, David trudged forward, believing in his calling, unwaveringly making life-changing
decisions almost daily. He lived what he wrote, "My hope is in
You all day long" (Ps. 25:5).

FAITH

Many of us have always looked to Hebrews 11:1 for our defini-
tion of faith: "Now faith is being sure of what we hope for and
certain of what we do not see."

Faith is part of our lives every single day, but God is known to
test us a little from time to time to make sure we have some and
that we are growing in this area. In other words, He stretches
us sometimes to check up on how much faith we really do have.
When it all works out, and we really do have just a little faith, it
is very exciting!

A few years ago, my good friend and wonderful singer, the
late Bobby Michaels, asked me to put a group together for his
upcoming musical outreach to Cuba in early September.

I gave the responsibility to one of our staff and forgot about it.
I knew this would be a fabulous opportunity and that all kinds
of singers would want to go. It was an easy recruit.

When mid-August rolled around, I asked the staff member
how it was going. "Not good," he replied. "There are no recruits
at all for Cuba." I couldn't believe it! I had committed to Bobby,
and he was counting on some vocal backup and another per-
forming group to give him some relief in the concerts he had set
up.

The end of our tour season was the next day. It left us no time to recruit or raise the necessary funds to send a team. I debated with myself for a few minutes about whether to cancel or find a way to move ahead. We had no time to have a group learn any music, let alone prepare it in Spanish. So we prayed that God would show us what to do and would give us the faith to do it.

CHILEAN CONTINENTALS

God brought our Chilean Continentals group to mind. I asked the staff member to call Gonzalo in Chile to see if he could put a small team together in two weeks. It would have been easier to quit, but it takes faith to move ahead when there seem to be no options. That was especially true with no funds to send them anywhere, even if we had the group.

We called the airlines to see what it would cost to send six people from Santiago to Havana. I was amazed to find out that the cost was hundreds of dollars less to go from Chile than from California.

> It would have been easier to quit, but it takes faith to move ahead when there seem to be no options.
>
> **7** SECRETS

The word came from Gonzalo: he had six great singers excited to go. Now all we needed was $2,500 to buy their tickets. The next morning was the final tour performance of one of our Young Continental Singers groups. I met one of the parents of this group, and she was so thrilled that she bounded up to me and said, "This has been such a wonderful experience for my daughter! I want to do something for you. Just tell me what you need."

So I told her we needed $2,500 to send six Chileans to
Havana for an incredible outreach with Bobby Michaels in Cuba.
She sat down, took out her checkbook, and wrote out a check for
that exact amount, right then and there. We were thrilled and
amazed at how quickly it all had happened. It took a little faith,
but God had intended all along that the Chileans would be a
much better choice for Cuba than a group from America who
couldn't speak or sing in Spanish.

We bought the tickets, and Gonzalo and his six singers were
off to Cuba! The results that Bobby shared later, along with
the reports from the Chileans, were beyond what any of us had
hoped or believed possible.

"Faith" is a noun—it is something we have. It is the firm belief
in something for which there is no proof. It is our big picture.
The Bible says that without faith, it is impossible to please God.
David operated by faith, flat-out 24/7, but he never used the
word "faith" in any of his writings. Still, he wrote these words
that describe his faith:

- "You are my God. My times are in Your hand…"
  (Ps. 31:14–15).

- "I cry out to God Most High, to God, who fulfills
  His purpose for me" (Ps. 57:2).

- "Our help is in the name of the Lord, the maker
  of heaven and earth" (Ps. 124:8).

- "With God, we will gain the victory" (Ps. 60:12).

"Faith" is a noun—it is something we have.

7 SECRETS

The action part of our faith is trust. Often, it feels like faith and trust are interchangeable, even though they are clearly different virtues.

TRUST

"Trust" is a verb—it is something we do. Trust is the response, the commitment to follow our faith into action.

I was a high-altitude mountaineer for many years, and having been at 21,000 feet, on a slippery glacier, with drop-offs on both sides, I learned firsthand that you have to have faith in your crampons, your ice axe, and in some cases, your partner. But you must trust that your steps are being placed carefully and that your balance is secure. Faith and trust are the right "technical stuff" to hang on to, and God is the right partner!

"Trust" is a verb—it is something we do.

7 SECRETS

Often in David's writings, he uses the word "trust," and it sounds like it's interchangeable with "faith." But these statements give him the courage and faith to move out, trusting for success.

David said, "Some trust in chariots and some in horses, but we trust in the name of the Lord our God" (Ps. 20:7) and "For the king trusts in the Lord" (Ps. 21:7). David combines his faith, his trust, his heart, and his song in Psalm 28:7 NIV: "The Lord is my strength and my shield; my heart trusts in Him, and I am helped. My heart leaps for joy, and I will give thanks to Him in song."

In this next story, David uses his faith and his trust in God and saves the day for his friends and family.

Ziglag (1 Sam. 29–30)

David had an unusual relationship with Achish, the King of Gath, the capitol of the Philistine empire. Philistia was a country on the Mediterranean coast west of Judah and southwest of Israel. How this friendship came about, no one knows. But David told his six hundred men that one of these days, Saul would likely catch up to them. The best thing they could do was escape to the land of the Philistines. That's what they did, and Saul gave up searching for them anywhere in Israel.

After making an agreement of some kind with Achish, David and his men moved their families to Gath. Living with the Philistines was just not that comfortable for him; after all, this is the city that Goliath had come from. So he asked Achish if he would give him a country town to live in so they would not be a bother to the king living in the royal city.

Achish agreed and gave him the town of Ziglag. From that time on, this town belonged to the kings of Judah. David and his men moved their families to Ziglag and lived there the last year and four months of his time of running from Saul.

Without Achish ever finding out, David and his band of men raided the nearby towns and villages of the Geshurites, Girzites, and Amalekites, taking home sheep, cattle, donkeys, camels, and clothes.

When Achish asked where he had been raiding, David always replied that they were in the Negev desert of Judah, Jerahmeel, and the Kenitees. This was so that Achish would think David had become odious to his people in Israel and would then be his servant forever.

Eventually, the Philistines gathered all their forces to attack Israel. While the Philistine commanders were marching with their units of hundreds and thousands, David and his men were marching in the rear with Achish. David seemed willing to go to battle against Saul, and Achish supported it, but the Philistine commanders were angry and felt David would turn on them in the middle of the battle and help Israel. Achish asked David to do nothing to displease the Philistine rulers and go back in peace. David and his men returned to Ziglag.

Disaster! While they were gone, an Amalekite raiding band had taken their wives and children captive, stolen their possessions, and burned their city! When David's men saw it, they wept aloud until their strength was gone, and some even considered stoning their leader.

David immediately went into action. Through Abiathar, his priest, he inquired of the Lord if he should pursue the Amalekites. He had faith in the answer, and it was positive: "Pursue them." Then he asked the Lord if he would overtake them. His answer: "You will overtake them and succeed in the rescue." David trusted the word from the Lord, and he and the six hundred men left immediately in pursuit.

They had already marched for three days to get home. Now they were moving even more quickly. Part of the way there, at a place called the Besor Ravine, two hundred men just could not go any farther.

They were left behind with supplies. The four hundred men who remained continued on until they found an Egyptian lying in the field. He was in bad shape. He hadn't eaten or had anything to drink in three days. David's men revived him with food and water and found out that he was a slave of one of the Amalekites. David asked him if he could lead them down to the raiding party. He made an agreement with David in exchange for his own life and led them down.

There they were, scattered across the countryside, eating, drinking, and reveling because of the great plunder they had taken from the Philistines and Judah. David and his men fought them from dusk that day, all night, until evening of the next day. Where they found the energy is more than we can understand, but these men were David's Mighty Men, their families were at stake, and none of the Amalekites escaped, except four hundred young men on camels.

1 Samuel 30:18–19 says, "David recovered everything the Amalekites had taken. Nothing was missing, young or old, boy or girl, plunder or anything else. David brought everything back, including all the herds of animals."

When they came to the two hundred men they left with the supplies, some of his men were adamant that they should not have a share in the plunder. But David instituted a law mandating that those who stay with the supplies are to get the same share as those who go down to battle. This is a concept still alive and well today.

Once they had returned to Ziglag, they rebuilt their town and sent shares of the plunder to the elders of Judah, who were David's friends, as a gift. They sent shares also to a list of fourteen cities all over Judah, "and to those in all the other places David and his men had roamed" (1 Sam. 30:31).

David was always more than generous. It was one of his best-loved virtues.

GENEROSITY

We all pretty much fall into one of two categories: givers or takers. I am pretty sure most of us would rather be around the giver types. In 2 Corinthians 9:7, we read, "God loves a cheerful giver." So it is not just the giving that counts, but the attitude that goes with it.

Way back thousands of years, God told Moses the standard he required: "This is what the Lord has commanded, from what you have, take an offering for the Lord.... And everyone who was willing and whose hearts moved him, came and brought an offering to the Lord" (Exod. 35:4–5, 21).

The apostle Paul reminded us of Jesus's words: "It is more blessed to give than to receive" (Acts 20:35).

Jesus proclaimed, "Give and it will be given to you. A good measure, pressed down, shaken together, and running over will be poured into your lap. For the measure you use, it will be measured to you" (Luke 6:38).

> We all pretty much fall into one of two categories: givers or takers.

7 SECRETS

Jesus also said more about this. In Matthew 10:8, He said, "Freely you have received, freely give." And in Matthew 6:21, he said, "For where your treasure is, there your heart will be also."

Where your heart is, and what's in it—well, that's what this little book is all about.

David wrote, "The righteous give generously" (Ps. 37:20).

David's giving was always over the top. At the end of his life, he had it in his heart to build a great temple for the name of the Lord in Jerusalem. But the prophet Nathan received word from God that David's son, Solomon, was to build the temple instead of David. He was a warring man, and Solomon was to be a king of peace.

David had been given all the plans for the construction of the temple from the Lord and delivered those to his son, Solomon. He also gave *all* of his personal treasure he had acquired from being king for forty years.

Speaking to all the leaders of Israel, David said, "Besides in my devotion to the temple of my God, I now give my personal treasures of gold and silver...over and above everything I have provided for this Holy temple; three thousand talents of gold (gold of ophir) and seven thousand talents of refined silver..." (1 Chron. 29:3).

According to the notes in my Bible, three thousand talents of gold is 110 tons of gold by today's standards, and seven thousand talents of silver would have been 260 tons of silver. I have no idea the number of carets that is involved here, but the gold of Ophir was extremely precious in that day, and the silver was refined.

Considering that there are 16 ounces in a pound and 2,000 pounds in a ton, each ton had 32,000 ounces. There was 110 tons of gold, which means David gave 3,520,000 ounces of gold. Using the same measure for the silver, he gave 8,320,000 ounces of silver.

While I am writing this, gold is at $1,216 an ounce (it has been a lot higher). At that rate, David gave $4,280,320,000 ($4.28 billion) in gold and just more than $428,179,000 million in silver, as well as massive amounts of bronze and precious stones.

The leaders of Israel followed his example and gave even more in total than David had given personally. Then he said these things to the Lord: "But who am I, and who are my people that we should be able to give as generously as this? Everything comes from You, and we have given You only what has come from Your hand. O Lord, our God, as for all this abundance, that we have provided for building You a temple for Your Holy Name, it comes from Your hand, and all of it belongs to You. *I know, my God, that You test the heart and are pleased with integrity. All these things I have given willingly and with honest intent*" (emphasis mine, 1 Chron. 29:14, 16–17).

David, like the widow who gave her copper pennies in Jesus's time would do, gave all his personal treasure. But that is not what God necessarily requires of our giving. He is more interested in our intent and our willingness. It is just about what is in our hearts.

If God really had a round table, would you be qualified to sit at it?

When raising funds for the church or other worthy Christian causes, people often respond, "I'll pray about it." David prayed about everything. His communication with the Lord was moment by moment. He called himself a man of prayer.

Three

LIVE IN THE MOMENT

DAVID'S SECRET #3

He Was a Man of Prayer

"I am a man of prayer" (David, Ps. 109:4).

"In the morning, O Lord, you hear my voice. In
the morning, I lay my requests before you and
wait in expectation" (David, Ps. 5:3).

"My Father will give you whatever you ask in My
name.... Ask and you will receive, and your joy
will be complete" (Jesus, John 16:23–24).

"Lord, listen to Your children praying.
Lord, send Your spirit in this place.
Lord, listen to Your children praying.
Send us love, send us power, send us grace."
—"LORD, LISTEN TO YOUR CHILDREN PRAYING,"
WORDS AND MUSIC BY KEN MEDEMA

DAVID WAS A man of prayer. Examining the 74 psalms
he wrote out of the 150, we can find his prayers on all
kinds of subjects. The theme of the ones I read most
often is that he pleads to God, "Save me from my enemies!" This
tells us he was always in the mode to trust God to rescue him
from one disaster or another. Though God surely knew his

troubles, David still wanted the Lord to know that he was asking for and expecting help. The Lord always came through for David.

Many great books have been written on the subject of prayer. They all agree that God receives blessing when we pray, and we receive blessings from Him in return, especially when we ask for them. This concept was made very clear to us in Bruce Wilkinson's wonderful book, *The Prayer of Jabez.* I have prayed that little prayer a thousand times or more, especially for my own children. I'm sure you have, too! God's word is full of promises, if we pray.

When God first looked at David's young heart, he already saw a man of prayer. As a shepherd, David must have learned to communicate with God when no one was around except the sheep. He had the time, and he had the Lord's awesome universe to gaze up at each clear night. I am sure it was out there, on the sides of those hills near Bethlehem, or off in some other green pastures in Judah, that David began to understand his Creator, and he loved talking with Him about all the things he could see.

> God receives blessing when we pray, and
> we receive blessings from Him in return,
> especially when we ask for them.

7 SECRETS

It was also out there in the hills that he became a professional slinger. And we can easily imagine him picking off any creature that bothered those sheep by using his sling and some small stones.

It is interesting to think of David as a shepherd. We sometimes prefer to think of him as the giant slayer, or the king who conquered every nation on his borders, or even the writer of great songs and lyrics, a hero in his own time. Being a shepherd seems like a really humble beginning and training ground for such a noble person. But that is how God does things so very often.

In W. Philip Keller's book, *A Shepherd Looks at Psalm 23*, we learn that a shepherd is a kind of hero to his sheep. Without the shepherd, a sheep is more likely to perish than to survive. And, of course, Jesus was called "The Good Shepherd." As a youth, David started out as a shepherd and then, understanding the role of a shepherd, he wrote Psalm 23: "The Lord is my Shepherd." It is probably the most loved of all the psalms.

PSALM 23

This psalm is unique. If you study it from David's life perspective, and some of his other writings, and what a shepherd really does, it brings on some new meanings. David wrote this psalm when he was still a young man. We don't know exactly the time, but it was most likely during the years that he was going from the pastures with his sheep to the palace to sing and play for Saul. In the first part of the psalm, he tells us what the Lord is doing for him. By the end, he is telling us what he is going to do for the Lord.

Included here are the lyrics to a song, "The Lord Is My Shepherd," from the musical *David, a Man After God's Own Heart*, which I wrote after I began to understand what I believe David was saying in Psalm 23. It has been called his "Impossible Dream" song, and it fits with his anointing as the future king by the prophet Samuel.

In the table below, the first column shows the *scripture*. The second column contains my *personal thoughts* about what David was saying. The third column contains the *lyrics of the song*, "The Lord Is My Shepherd," words by Cam Floria and music by Ronna Jordan.

The Scripture (Ps. 23, NIV)	My Personal Thoughts about What David Was Saying	The Song Lyrics
The Lord is my shepherd.	The Lord is my guide, my leader, mentor, pastor, trusted friend.	"The Lord is my shepherd, my trusted friend and guide."
I shall not be in want.	So I don't need anything, He takes care of me. I don't have to worry about anything. I just need him. He's always by my side.	"I don't need anything; He's always there. He takes care of me."
He makes me lie down in green pastures.	He puts me in places and situations that have life! Real possibilities for growth. Places that are growing and alive with people who think right, who want to make a difference. He gives me beautiful places to stay, pleasant places to live, and plenty to eat. He sees to my physical needs. He puts me in the right and best place at just the right and best time.	"He makes me walk in pleasant places; green pastures."
He leads me beside quiet waters.	He takes me to quiet places, where I can easily be filled with His Spirit. He leads me to lovely streams and beautiful green mountain lakes where I can think, strategize, and gain spiritual strength. He knows what it does to me.	"And by the quiet streams, mountain lakes, and still waters…."
He restores my soul.	This does restore my own spirit, especially when I've been giving and giving. He always finds a way to restore my spirit so that I can catch my second wind and feel invigorated again.	"He restores me."

The Scripture (Ps. 23, NIV)	My Personal Thoughts about What David Was Saying	The Song Lyrics
He guides me in paths of righteousness for His name's sake.	He guides me along a path, a trail that will accomplish His will, what He has in mind. He helps me make the right decisions and the right choices because I ask Him to, in His Name. I want His direction to be my direction. A path that will not fail. I'm traveling along a path He has selected. I'm following His trail, in His footsteps.	"He guides me along a path of righteousness, a path He chose for His namesake."
Even though I walk through the valley of the shadow of death....	When things get tough and the opposition is strong, even when failure looms on every side, even if I face the hardest and most difficult challenge in my life, a dark shadow....	"And, if I face the hardest, most difficult challenge in my life, the darkest shadow, my darkest hour...."
I will fear no evil, for You are with me.	I won't be afraid of any difficulty or problem, no matter how big it is. I won't be afraid of anything or anyone. Because You are with me, I can do anything, go anywhere, climb any mountain with You as my guide.	"I will not be afraid of anyone. I'll go anywhere. Because You are with me, I can do anything."
Your rod and Your staff, they comfort me.	Your word and Your spirit give me courage, and strength, faith, and comfort.	"Your Words and Your Spirit give me courage, give me comfort, give me strength."

The Scripture (Ps. 23, NIV)	My Personal Thoughts about What David Was Saying	The Song Lyrics
You prepare a table before me in the presence of my enemies.	You give me great ideas and make me successful right in front of people who are sure I will fail, who want me to fail. You pour out blessings right in the middle of what seems to be sure disaster, when some are hoping for the worst, for my destruction.	"You're preparing a wonderful future; a purpose, a vict'ry in front of my enemies, people who say I'm sure to fail, who think I'm too weak, not worthy of You."
You anoint my head with oil; my cup overflows.	You have anointed me, chosen me, given me a destiny, and the blessings and good things overflow. They just keep coming, and no one can stop them.	"But You have anointed me, given me a destiny, opened my eyes to see. You have chosen me."
Surely goodness and love will follow me all the days of my life.	Surely happiness, fulfillment, abundance, and love will be mine for the rest of my life. How privileged, how loved, and how special I feel because You have blessed my life.	"And Your blessings and perfect gifts will continually overflow. Surely goodness will follow me; Your love will cover my life!"

The Scripture (Ps. 23, NIV)	My Personal Thoughts about What David Was Saying	The Song Lyrics
And I will dwell in the house of the Lord forever.	And I will always live to serve You, to accomplish Your plans for my life, and to live out my destiny. All I am and all I have is Yours forever.	"And I will always live for You, to be close to You, following You. Because all that I am, and all that I will ever be, is Yours, forever. I'm Yours, forever! I am Yours!"

JESUS WAS ALSO A MAN OF PRAYER

As we read about Jesus in the Gospel, we see that His preferred place for prayer was off in the mountains, in the wilderness, or in a solitary place. These are the same kinds of places David learned to pray.

The disciples were normal, secular businesspeople, and in the beginning, they didn't know how to pray. So they asked Jesus how to pray. In Matthew, chapter 6, and again in Luke, chapter 11, Jesus taught them what we now know as "The Lord's Prayer." Later, these same people were able to change their world and ours, through prayer and faith, watching God answer their prayers, through His power.

Jesus told us again and again, if we ask anything in His name, it will be given to us. "If you believe," He said, "you will receive whatever you ask for in prayer." But James, Jesus' brother, warned us in his epistle that if we prayed with the wrong motive, we would not receive what we asked for (Matt. 21:12).

Jesus warned His disciples about promoting their spirituality in their public prayers. He used the religious leaders of His day, the Pharisees, as an example of that kind of motivation. That is why He said, "But when you pray, go into your room, close the door, and pray to your Father, Who is unseen. Then, your Father, Who sees what is done in secret, will reward you.... Your Father knows what you need before you ask Him" (Matt. 6:6, 8).

David said something similar: "May the words of my mouth and the meditation of my heart be pleasing in your sight, O Lord, my Rock and my Redeemer" (Ps. 19:4).

> Jesus told us again and again, if we ask anything in His name, it will be given to us.

7 SECRETS

For all of us, prayer can become a ritual, like at mealtime. We pray because it is expected, yet if we are truly thankful, think what a blessing that is to the Lord. I have to admit that our prayer at mealtimes varies. Sometimes, we pray at the beginning, like we all learned was correct. But then, in this crazy life, where everyone is running too fast and life seems to be ruled by cell phones, social media, soccer, and other related good things, the pause to be thankful might be in the middle or at the end of the meal. God doesn't care, if we are truly thankful, and He is the only judge of that!

Just out of college and working with Youth for Christ (YFC), I heard a story about a well-known Youth for Christ speaker from Detroit named Don Loney. Some of the YFC leaders had gathered for a meeting. Afterward, they all went out for pie and ice cream.

When the food came, Loney said, "Let's pray!" All the guys looked a bit surprised and said that they had already prayed and thanked God for the dessert. Loney called those kind of prayers "fuss with your napkin prayers." So he stood up, folded his napkin neatly on the seat of his chair, got down on his knees, and prayed loudly enough for the entire restaurant to hear. Not only did he thank God for the food; he prayed for *all* the missionaries in Africa!

There are times, for sure, when prayers in front of large groups are certainly mesmerizing and glorifying to God. We just have to remember those thousands of people gathering at so many Billy Graham Crusades all over the world, who responded to the prayer of salvation to receive Jesus Christ as their personal Savior.

The point is, one of the secrets to becoming a person after God's heart is to become a person of prayer. Prayers are not necessarily like those of Rolly, a friend of my family, who prayed in a different voice than he spoke. It was kind of ultra-religious, with a big, hollow, slow, holy sound. It actually scared me as a kid. But it's better to pray in your own voice, a real prayer, from your own heart.

> One of the secrets to becoming
> a person after God's heart is to
> become a person of prayer.

7 SECRETS

Here is an idea for you. There is a great book of collected teachings called *Practice the Presence of God* compiled by Father Joseph de Beaufort and written by a Carmelite Monk named Brother Lawrence, who lived in the mid 1600's. The idea is that you talk to God in conversation, practicing the idea—actually the truth—that He is right there in the same room with you or in the seat next to you in your car, or walking down the sidewalk beside you. Actually, it works anywhere! My favorite place is being seated on a lava-rock cliff, knowing He is there, too, listening to the crash of the ocean below and watching one of His magnificent sunsets. My golden retriever, Maverick, also sitting there, keeps reacting like he is the one being talked to. We can talk in our minds as well, but this really works. The title of the book is the giveaway: "practice!" If this is a new idea for you, you will see how practicing God's presence, wherever you are, helps you pray continually and keeps you on track in your Christian life.

If we learn anything from David about being a person of prayer, it is that all subjects are OK to pray about. He prayed when things were good and when they were difficult; when he was joyful and when he was terrified and afraid. We can do the same.

Here are some phrases from his prayers found in the psalms, when his father-in-law, King Saul, sent men to his house to kill him. He wrote, "Deliver me from my enemies, O God; protect me from those who rise up against me....I have done no wrong, yet they are ready to attack me. Arise to help me" (Ps. 59:1, 4).

While hiding in a cave from Saul, David cried out, "Have mercy on me, O God, have mercy on me, for in You my soul takes refuge. I will take refuge in the shadow of Your wings until the disaster has passed....I am in the midst of lions!" (Ps. 57:1, 4).

When the Philistines had seized him in Gath, David said, "When I am afraid, I will trust in You. In God, whose word I praise, in God I trust; I will not be afraid. What can mortal man do to me?... For You have delivered me from death and my feet from stumbling, that I may walk before the Lord in the light of life" (Ps. 56:3–4, 13).

When God's promise through Samuel was finally realized, and David was through with caves and years of running and hiding, all the things he had learned about fighting and warring came into play while leading the armies of Israel. A couple of stories in 2 Samuel, chapter 5, reveal that David always sought the Lord before marching off to war. He had just been named King of Israel, and of course, the Philistines decided to hit him hard before the kingdom was well established, after the seven years of civil war between Judah and Israel.

So they mounted two large-scale attacks on Israel. About the first one David reported, "As water breaks out, the Lord has broken out against my enemies before me." He defeated them the first time. It's the second battle that is the focus of our next story.

MARCHING IN THE TOPS OF THE TREES (2 SAM. 5:20, 22–25)

"Once more, the Philistines came up and spread out in the valley of Rephaim, so David inquired of the Lord...." He prayed that the Lord would direct him in this critical battle and give Israel the victory.

David knew the strategies of war after all those years of fighting, but this time, he listened to God's strategy. The Lord answered, "Do not go straight up," like the normal battles lines were formed, "but circle around behind them in front of the balsam trees. As soon as you hear the sound of marching in the tops of the balsam trees, move quickly, because that will mean the Lord has gone out in front of you to strike the Philistine army."

So David and his army outflanked the Philistine army and circled around behind, probably at night, until they reached the other side of the balsam forest, which was now between them and the enemy. They waited....

Then they heard it! Off in the distance, whoo, whoo, whoo, whoo, growing louder: *WHOO, WHOO, WHOO, WHOO.* It was the army of the Lord, thundering in step through the tops of the trees! Breathing stopped! Fear gripped! Chills ran up and down arms! Adrenaline spiked! Swords flashed out of scabbards! They rushed out into the dark forest to meet the enemy!

"So David did as the Lord commanded him, and he struck

down the Philistines all the way from Gibeon to Gezer!" Whew, what a powerful weapon is prayer in the hands of a man of prayer! As James 5:16 declares, "The prayer of a righteous man is powerful and effective."

Here are some other random verses and phrases from David's prayers found throughout the psalms. These are the same kinds of things you might pray when the circumstances in your life cause you to turn to the Lord.

- "Arise, O Lord! Deliver me, O my God! Strike all my enemies on the jaw; break the teeth of the wicked" (Well, maybe..., Ps. 3:7).

- "Keep me as the apple of Your eye; hide me in the shadow of Your wings" (Ps. 17:8).

- "O Lord, You have seen this, be not silent. Do not be far from me, O Lord" (Ps. 35:12).

- "May Your blessing be on Your people" (Ps. 3:8).

- "Turn to me and be gracious to me, for I am lonely and afflicted. The troubles of my heart have multiplied..." (Ps. 25:16–17).

- "Let the light of Your face shine upon us, O Lord" (Ps. 4:6).

- "Hear my cry, O God; listen to my prayer. From the ends of the earth I call to You. I call as my heart grows faint; lead me to the Rock that is higher than I" (Ps. 61:1–2).

- "Show the wonder of Your great love..." (Ps. 17:7).

- "Do not hide Your face from Your servant; answer me quickly, for I am in trouble" (Ps. 69:17).

+ "Pray for the peace of Jerusalem; may those who love You be secure, may there be peace within Your walls and security within Your citadels" (Ps. 122:6–7). (It's OK to pray for peace in the world and for security in our nation.)

+ "Set a guard over my mouth, O Lord. Keep watch over the door of my lips. Let not my heart be drawn to what is evil, to take part in wicked deeds with men who are evildoers; let me not eat of their delicacies" (Ps. 41:3–4). This is similar to the Lord's Prayer: "And lead us not into temptation, but deliver us from the evil one" (Matt. 6:13).

+ "My eyes are fixed on You, O sovereign Lord" (Ps. 141:8).

David's prayers were stimulated by the situations he found himself in at the time. Most of his prayers start with a difficult circumstance, but they almost always end in praise, worship, and thanks.

In the Lord's Prayer, Jesus starts with recognizing God's awesome holiness, then asks for deliverance. Our circumstances, too, will dictate how we need to pray.

But what about getting answers to your prayers? So often it can feel like God is just not listening or really doesn't seem to care. You can remember the taunts of the prophet Elijah to the prophets of Baal when their prayers to burn up the sacrifice on the altar were not answered. Elijah sarcastically said, "Shout louder...maybe He is sleeping." Then God answered Elijah's prayer by burning the entire water-doused altar, along with the sacrifice in one of the most profound answers to prayer in the whole Bible (1 Kings 18:27).

> Most of his prayers start with a difficult
> circumstance, but they almost always
> end in praise, worship, and thanks.

7 SECRETS

Even David was sometimes frustrated and distraught when God's answer to his pleading was not immediate. He said, "Turn, O Lord, and deliver me. Save me because of Your unfailing love. No one remembers you when he is dead. Who praises You from the grave? I am worn out from groaning." Pretty extreme, huh? Then he realizes God has heard him and says, "The Lord has heard my cry for mercy. The Lord accepts my prayer"! (Ps. 6:4–6a, 9).

What about you? Have you ever had an immediate answer to a prayer? This kind of confirmation from the Lord is more than wonderful. It's a powerful recognition that you are really heard. It's humbling, emotional, and beautiful, all at once. It doesn't happen like that very often, but if it ever happened to you, even once, you would never doubt again that God is always really listening. His timing is often not our timing, but it has happened to me on a few occasions. I needed to know I was being heard, and the Lord was willing to give me an immediate answer.

> Have you ever had an immediate answer
> to a prayer? This kind of confirmation
> from the Lord is more than wonderful.

7 SECRETS

One such occasion was one of those times in my life when I was struggling with the question "Why is this happening to me?" Like I do so often to get in touch with the Lord and my feelings, I went into the mountains here on Kauai. I walked the trails, looking at the beautiful views for miles and miles along the ridges in the forest. All day, with the ocean way out there ahead of me, I was praying, listening, meditating, crying, feeling bad for myself, praising anyway some of the time, just having a mouthful of "whys," and needing some answers.

Finally, I arrived to one of my absolute favorite spots, a great clearing in the middle of the jungled forest. It was near sunset, and the coming greyness creeping up from below was now being overcome by the dancing orange and yellow colors that were spreading over the tops of the trees. It was the end of the day, and not far up the trailhead would be my car and a drive home. There had been no answers to my pleading. No confirmations that I was being heard, and now it was almost over. I was weary, but my spirit was full anyway, like only those times can bring.

I stopped near the end of the clearing and said to the Lord, "I realize I don't have the right to test You, Lord, and I can't just expect that You will always answer my prayers and desires like I want. But if You could, just this one time, let me know You at least heard me today and know and understand the pain in my heart. Well, I apologize, but I would be so very grateful."

Then I took just a few steps, and a beautiful doe walked out into the path just ahead of me, maybe twenty-five feet. She stopped and looked at me, her ears flipped, her eyes met mine, and then she calmly walked into the forest on the other side of the trail.

There was no question in my spirit that the appearance of that doe where she would normally never be was God's answer that He had been listening and cared about my situation. It was the confirmation I needed, and it changed everything for me right then. I never doubt that God is listening, but like most of us, I am still impatient enough to hope for some kind of quick answer! God's timing or ours—it doesn't matter when you know He is listening.

In John 14, Jesus prayed for His disciples. In John 17:20, He prayed for us, too. Think about the power of that! "My prayer is not for them alone; I pray also for those who will believe in Me through their message." That, my friends, is *you* and *me*, if we believe in Him!

Prayer is conversation with God, the Lord, our Heavenly Father, on our terms, in our own way. The same as it was for David. Practice the presence of God, and when you pray, just know He is there, too!

One of the greatest prayers of all time was prayed by the apostle Paul for the Ephesians at the end of chapter 3. He kneels before the Father in heaven and prays that His glorious riches will strengthen those Ephesians with His power so that they can grasp how wide, long, high, and deep is the love of Christ. He ends his prayer with this great promise that is just as much for us as it was for them: "Now to Him who is able to do immeasurably more than all we ask or imagine, according to His power that is at work within us, to Him be glory in the church and in Christ Jesus throughout all generations, forever and ever! Amen!" (Eph. 3:14–21).

> Prayer is conversation with God,
> the Lord, our Heavenly Father, on
> our terms, in our own way.

7 SECRETS

What do you think the scripture means when it says, "Pray continually"?

David was a man of prayer. Yet one of his most serious times of prayer included remorse, forgiveness, and repentance. It is one of the reasons his story remains so very powerful—because he humbled himself and was willing to take the heat for the consequences of his sin.

Four

TAKE THE HEAT

DAVID'S SECRET #4

He Was a Man of Repentance and Forgiveness

"You are forgiving and good, O Lord, abounding in
love to all who call to You" (David, Ps. 86:5).

"Forgive us our sins, for we also forgive everyone who
sins against us" (The Lord's Prayer, Jesus, Luke 11:4).

"It is no secret what God can do,
What He's done for others, He'll do for you.
With arms wide open, He'll pardon you.
It is no secret, what God can do."
—"IT IS NO SECRET," WORDS AND
MUSIC BY STUART HAMBLEN

THE IMPORTANCE OF forgiveness in our lives is no secret.
But those simple little words, "I am sorry" or "I forgive
you," are so hard for some to say and really mean. Yet
that type of expression is one of the great essentials of becoming
a man or a woman after God's heart!

PART ONE: ABIGAIL AND BEYOND

It was a time of raiding bands of ruthless men who killed, burned,
racked other villages and ranches, carried off prisoners, and took
all the bounty back to their own cities and camps.

Wealthy ranchers either had their own small militia of mer-
cenaries or gave supplies to other roving bands to pay for protection. David had such a band of men.

According to 1 Samuel chapter 25, David and his men had
been protecting one of the most successful ranchers of that time,
a man named Nabal. He had one thousand goats and three
thousand sheep. At the end of the season, he was shearing his
sheep near Carmel.

Hearing that it was shearing time, and knowing Nabal would
be celebrating, David sent ten young men up to greet Nabal, to
honor him with kind words for success, and to ask for whatever
supplies Nabal would be willing to give to his protectors. Nabal
was known as a man who was surly and mean in his dealings with
others. His response was as his reputation warranted: "Who is
this David?" Nabal growled. "Why should I take my bread and
water, and the meat I have slaughtered for my shearers, and give
it to men coming from who knows where?" He sent them away
empty-handed.

When this was reported to David, his response was instant:
"Put on your swords!" He took four hundred of his men and
headed straight for Nabal's shearing camp. David was angry.
This was a feeling David knew well from his years serving Saul
and his household. "It has been useless," he said, "watching over
this fellow's property." He felt Nabal was paying him back evil
for the good he had done.

Abigail was known as one of the most beautiful and intelligent
women in her part of the world. She had everything a woman
could ever want—servants, riches, position, honor. And she was
married to Nabal. One of Nabal's servants told Abigail that
David had sent messengers to Nabal to ask for supplies and that
her husband had hurled insults at them. The servant went on
to say, "Night and day, they were a wall around us, all the time

while we were herding the sheep near them. Now...disaster is hanging over our master and his whole household."

Abigail lost no time. She took two hundred loaves of bread, two skins of wine, five dressed sheep, five containers of roasted grain, a hundred cakes of raisins, and two hundred cakes of pressed figs and loaded them on donkeys. She got on her donkey and told the servant, "Go on ahead; I will follow you." But she did not tell her husband, Nabal.

When Abigail saw David, she quickly got off her donkey and bowed down before him with her face to the ground. "My Lord, let the blame be on me alone," she said. "And let this gift, which your servant has brought to my master, be given to the men who follow you. Please forgive your servant's offense, for the Lord will certainly make a lasting dynasty for my master and has appointed him leader over Israel."

Abigail's words were a great relief and joy to David's heart, just as his were to her. "Praise be to the Lord, the God of Israel," he said. "May you be blessed for your good judgment and for keeping me from avenging myself with my own hands. Go home in peace. I have heard your words and granted your request."

Pardoned, she went home. When she arrived, Nabal was holding a banquet. He was in high spirits but very drunk. In the morning, when he was sober, she told him all the things that had happened. His heart failed him, and he became like a stone. Ten days later, he died.

Pardoned, forgiven, being set free, the pressure is released, whether we are asking for mercy and pardon or we are being asked for the same. It may be between us and our Creator, or perhaps a friend, family member, associate, or someone else in our world.

I remember so clearly a sweet young Japanese couple, leaders of a Continentals Singers ministry in Japan, who came to a director's retreat in Colorado some years ago. With tears streaming down her face, Shoko surprised us all by apologizing on behalf of her country for what had happened during World War II. Even though this incident happened long before she was born, it seemed somehow necessary for her personal cleansing in a spiritual retreat with a group of young Americans. Lots of hugs and tears confirmed to Shoko that she was loved and certainly forgiven.

We can look at these distinct parts of the forgiveness formula in this way:

1. First, recognize our wrongdoing, then accept and own it.

2. Ask for forgiveness. This may involve an apology with humility and with remorse.

3. Accept the forgiveness being offered by the one we have offended. Sometimes this is the most difficult, yet most critical part.

4. Repent, which includes the commitment to make a change of heart necessary to move forward.

Second chances are possible.

But what about forgiving when no one is asking for it? Hanging on the cross, Jesus said, in Luke 23:34, "Father, forgive them, for they do not know what they are doing." No one was asking.

Second chances are possible.

7 SECRETS

When David was serving in Saul's court, rumors accused him of disloyalty to the king. Psalm 35 is full of David's feelings about these accusations. He said, "They hid their net for me without cause, and, without cause, dug a pit for me. Ruthless witnesses come forward; they question me on things I know nothing about. They repay me evil for good. They slandered me without ceasing."

What about someone who does not want to forgive when they have been wronged? After many struggles, a certain young woman, abused by her father in every kind of way, became a Christian. When she heard that her father had repented and accepted Christ moments before he died, her initial feeling was a wish that he had gone to his punishment rather than being forgiven. Of course she repented of that wish!

Once, being wrongly accused by a friend, I called and asked his forgiveness anyway. There seemed to be no way to change his heart. His response was, "That changes nothing."

As a young man, when David was learning about these things, he asked his friend, Jonathan, Saul's son, "What have I done? What is my crime? How have I wronged your father that he is trying to take my life?" In 1 Samuel 20:1, Jonathan assured David he had done no wrong, but David had to flee for his life anyway.

David's attitude about this is very clear in Psalm 37: "Wait for the Lord and keep His way. He will exalt you! Trust in the Lord and do good and enjoy safe pasture. Delight yourself in the Lord, and He will give you the desires of your heart. Commit you way to the Lord; trust in Him, and...He will make your righteousness shine like the dawn, the justice of your cause like the noonday sun."

David understood pardon and forgiveness to a depth most of us will never understand nor experience. In his book, [*David the Poet and King*], published in 1900, author Newell Dwight Hillis wrote these uncluttered yet purely honest words, unaffected by contemporary thinking, about David:

David has been earth's wisest teacher regarding remorse, penitence, faith, and pardon. Our libraries hold the confessions of Augustine, Rousseau, and of Tolstoy. But no man has dealt more sternly with himself than David.

His pages are thick with the expressions "My transgressions," "My iniquity," and "My sins." Made soft by luxury, weakened by flattery, in an evil hour, David yields to his passions, and sin sweeps through his life like a conflagration sweeping through a city and leaving only blackened timbers and ashes behind. Then comes the swift, sharp repentance, the open restitution, the instant and public confession, the self-abasement, the years of pain, the psalms and prayers that plead for man's pity and for God's pardon.

Never was there a more lovable youth! Never a career so rich and romantic!

Never a man who climbed so high and fell so low!

Never one whose repentance was more absolute and all-inclusive.

Never had one who fought his way so persistently back toward the heights where good men dwell.

PART TWO: BATHSHEBA AND BEYOND

It was spring when kings went off to war, but King David decided to stay at home this time. He had finally subdued the Philistines, whom he had been fighting for half his life. He was somewhere around forty-eight to fifty years old now and was just ready for some down time away from the noise and fatigue of the battle.

Other wars were still going on, however, and David sent Joab, his general, out with his men and the entire Israeli army. They destroyed the Ammonites and were besieging their main city,

Rabbah. But David was enjoying Jerusalem's beautiful spring in the palace.

One evening, David got up from his bed and took a walk on the roof of the palace. There, he looked down on a beautiful woman bathing. David sent someone to find out about her, who returned to report that her name was Bathsheba and that she was married to Uriah, the Hittite.

David knew Uriah. He was one of his thirty mighty men, who at that moment was engaged in the battle with the Ammonites at Rabbah. David sent a messenger to bring Bathsheba to him anyway.

One wonders if had he met Bathsheba previously and did not recognize her from the roof in the evening twilight. Did she know of David's habit of walking on the roof in the evening? The bottom line, however, is that it makes no difference. Passion took over, and they slept together that evening. She became pregnant.

Once David found out that Bathsheba was going to have a child, he sent for Uriah and began to stage his cover-up plan. He told Uriah to go home, take a few nights off, and be with his wife. But Uriah, being loyal to his comrades in arms, refused to go to his wife while others were still in the battle for Rabbah.

So, the next evening, David invited him to dinner and made sure that Uriah had plenty of wine. Again, David sent him to his wife. When Uriah refused again, David sent him back to his general, Joab. In a note to the general, David told Joab to put Uriah where the strongest defenders were, and then to pull his troops back so that Uriah would be killed.

And that's exactly how it happened!

As soon as the time of mourning was over, Bathsheba became David's wife, and in time, their baby was born. No one knows for sure how much time passed before Nathan, the prophet, came to David with a word from the Lord. Most scholars guess that the baby was about a year old. Nathan told David an amazing story in 2 Samuel chapter 12. It is one of the most brilliant word pictures ever written.

The story is about two men in a certain town; one was rich and the other poor. The rich man had a large number of sheep and cattle, but the poor man had nothing, except for one little ewe lamb. The lamb grew up with the poor man and his children. It shared his food, drank from his cup, and even slept in his arms. It was like a daughter to him.

A traveler came to the rich man, but instead of taking one of his own sheep or cattle to prepare a meal for his friend, he took the ewe lamb that belonged to the poor man and prepared it for the traveler who had come to him.

"David burned with anger against the man in the story and said to Nathan, 'As surely as the Lord lives, the man who did this deserves to die!'"

Then Nathan said to David, "You are the man!" He went on to recount from the Lord all the great blessings the Lord had poured down on David. Then came two disastrous consequences for his sin. "Now, therefore, the sword will never depart from your house. Out of your own house I am going to bring calamity upon you." David humbled himself and said, "I have sinned against the Lord."

Nathan replied, "The Lord has taken away your sin. You are not going to die, but because by doing this you have made the enemies of the Lord show utter contempt, the son born to you will die" (2 Samuel 12:5, 7, 10–11, 13–14).

A third horrible consequence.

David was stunned. He went before the Lord and lay prostrate on the ground weeping, admitting his guilt, asking for God's mercy for his new son. He did not eat or drink for seven days.

After the seventh day, he noticed his servants whispering and realized his son had died. "Is the child dead?" he asked.

"Yes," they replied, "the child is dead."

Then David got up from the ground. After he had washed himself, put on lotions, and changed his clothes, he went into the house of the Lord and worshipped (2 Sam. 12:19–20).

It is striking to realize that in the discovery and judgment of his greatest sin, David was moved to go into the presence of the Lord and worship. The only answer can be that He knew he was forgiven, even though he didn't deserve it. God's forgiveness is ours, too, just for the asking. The apostle Paul went so far as to say that we are saved and forgiven by God's grace through faith. It is not of ourselves; it is God's free gift, so that no one can boast that he earned it.

All during the time he was silent, the Lord was convicting David of his wrongdoing. He writes in Psalm 32:3–5, "When I kept silent, my bones wasted away through my groaning all day long, for day and night Your hand was heavy upon me, my strength was sapped. Then I acknowledged my sin to You and did not cover up my iniquity, and You forgave the guilt of my sin."

> It is striking to realize that in the discovery and judgment of his greatest sin, David was moved to go into the presence of the Lord and worship.

7 SECRETS

In Psalm 38, he says again, "My guilt has overwhelmed me like a burden too heavy to bear…because of my sinful folly. I am bowed down and brought very low; all day long I go about mourning…even the light has gone from my eyes." And after more of these descriptions, he says, "I confess my iniquity and am troubled by my sin" (Ps. 38:4–6, 10, 18).

The famous Psalm 51 has a notation: "A psalm of David when

the prophet Nathan came to him after David had committed adultery with Bathsheba."

David wrote, "Have mercy on me, O God, according to Your unfailing love, according to Your great compassion, blot out my transgressions. Wash away all my iniquity and cleanse me from my sin.... Cleanse me with Hyssop, and I will be clean; wash me and I will be whiter than snow. Let me hear joy and gladness; let the bones you have crushed rejoice. Hide Your face from my sins, and blot out all my iniquity. Create in me a pure heart, O God, and renew a steadfast spirit within me. Do not cast me from Your presence or take Your Holy Spirit from me. Restore me to the joy of Your salvation, and grant me a willing spirit to sustain me" (Ps. 51:1–2, 7–12).

That is an amazing flow of words from a broken heart and a contrite spirit. But there is always a price to pay for our sin. It is a good thing the Bible says in 1 John 1:9, "If we confess our sins, He is faithful and just and will forgive us our sins and purify us from all unrighteousness."

Hillis again writes in his ancient book these powerful and provocative words:

> Coarse men and unthinking have despised David for his crimes, and confessed surprise that his songs are in the Psalter, and that history has made a place for David among the heroes of faith. Ignorance and shallowness may sneer that the gifted poet made up for black crime by psalms, and that God thinks lightly of foul sins, since these songs, red with blood and black with guilt, are bound up in his Bible. But the sneer is both super-ficial and unjust. The great epic dramas are less than a score in number, and all are based upon some expe-rience to David's. In jurisprudence we mention Moses.
>
> Now Moses was a murderer. In literature, no writing is more famous than Paul's ode to 'the love that never

fails.' But Paul's garments were stained with Stephen's blood. From David to Paul, the heroes are not soft youths lingering on languorous violet beds.

They are knights pushing their way into the thick of the battle, and either slaying sin or carried off the field upon their shields.

While visiting Israel and being in Jerusalem for some time a few years ago, I was astonished to learn that the most revered name from Israel's past is not Abraham, who was promised that his descendants would be like the stars in the universe and the sand on the seashore, nor Moses, who led the Israelites out of Egypt.

> There is always a price to pay for our sin.

7 SECRETS

No, it is David. The young, peasant shepherd boy who became court minstrel, the chosen favorite of the prince, champion of Goliath and the army, a conquering hero, object of the people's songs, rival of the king, and upon taking the throne, the one who became the worship leader of a nation, Israel's singer of songs, commercial leader, statesman, mighty warrior who conquered every nation on his border and others far away. Through his leadership, Israel rose to its greatest height in the world of that day. This is the David who Israel remembers and reveres today.

The story of David is the perfect example of how forgiveness works between man and God, and between man and other men and women. It is one of the most important reasons his story is still alive, vibrant, and necessary for today.

"There is no one who does good, not even one." David wrote this in Psalm 14:3 and again in Psalm 53:3. When the apostle Paul wrote the same in Romans 3:10, he was quoting David. Paul continues in the third chapter of Romans, verse 23: "For all have sinned and fall short of the glory of God." As a result, we all need forgiveness, and we all need to be able to forgive. Jesus said it simply in Luke 6:37: "Forgive and you will be forgiven."

In the traditional version of the Lord's Prayer, Jesus taught his disciples to pray, "Forgive us our trespasses (debts) as we forgive those who trespass against us," or as one little four-year-old prayed: "And forgive us our trash baskets as we forgive those who put trash in our baskets." Well, I guess we could say that sin is trash in our basket, and forgiving is the answer to emptying our basket (Matt. 6:12, 14–15, KJV).

Finally, David talks about the promise of forgiveness in the greatest testimony yet for all of us to hold onto in Psalm 103: "Praise the Lord, O my soul, and forget not all His benefits, who forgives all your sins. The Lord is compassionate and gracious, slow to anger, abounding in love. He does not treat us as our sins deserve, or repay us according to our iniquities.

For as high as the heavens are above the earth, so great is His love for those who fear Him; as far as the East is from the West, so far has He removed our transgressions from us (Ps. 103:2, 8, 10–12).

> The story of David is the perfect
> example of how forgiveness works
> between man and God, and between
> man and other men and women.

7 SECRETS

If there is someone you need to forgive or ask forgiveness of, will you consider doing so this week?

David had to forgive and be forgiven. Yet through all his struggles, he never wavered in loving God the way God intended, with *all* his heart and *all* his strength.

Five

ALL

DAVID'S SECRET #5

He Loved God with All His Heart and All His Strength

"I love You, O Lord, my strength" (David, Ps. 18:1).

"Love the Lord your God with all your heart, and with all your soul, and with all your strength" (God, Deut. 6:5).

> "If with all your heart ye truly seek Me,
> Ye shall ever surely find Me,
> Thus saith our God."
> —"ELIJAH" BY FELIX MENDELSSOHN

> "I love You, Lord.
> And I lift my voice,
> To worship You,
> O, my soul, rejoice.
> Take joy, my King,
> In what You hear,
> Let it be a sweet, sweet,
> Sound in Your ear."
> —"I LOVE YOU, LORD," WORDS AND
> MUSIC BY LAURIE KLEIN

THE RECORDED LOVE relationship between David and the Lord started when God looked into David's heart as a teenager and saw all the things about him that we have been discussing in this book. David was faithful to his calling, from that time throughout his entire life, and talked about how much he loved God all the time.

In 2 Samuel 7, the writer lays out a beautiful story of David's love relationship with God from his later years. The King of Tyre floated some cedar logs down the Mediterranean and provided workers who built the palace for his friend, King David. "After David was settled in the palace, and the Lord had given him rest from all his enemies around him, he said to Nathan the prophet, 'Here, I am living in a palace of cedar, while the ark of God remains in a tent.'" Nathan replied to the king, "Whatever you have in mind, go ahead and do it, for the Lord is with you."

That night, the word of the Lord came to Nathan, saying, "Go and tell my servant David, 'This is what the Lord says: Are you the one to build me a house to dwell in? I have been moving from place to place with a tent as my dwelling. Whenever I have moved with all the Israelites, did I ever say to any of their rulers, "Why have you not built Me a house of cedar?"'

"Now then, tell my servant David, 'This is what the Lord Almighty says: I took you from the pasture and from following the flock to be ruler over My people, Israel. I have been with you wherever you have gone, and I have cut off all your enemies from before you. Now, I will make your name great, like the names of the greatest men of the earth.'" Whew!

"The Lord declares to you that the Lord himself will establish a house for you. When your days are over and you rest with your fathers, I will raise up your offspring to succeed you, who will come from your own body... [*It was to be Solomon*]. He is the one who will build a house for my *name*" (emphasis mine).

"Your house and your kingdom will endure forever before Me; before me, your throne will be established forever."

Then King David sat before the Lord and said, "Who am I, O Sovereign Lord, and what is my family, that You have brought me this far? And, as if this were not enough in Your sight, O Sovereign Lord, You have also spoken about the future of the house of Your servant.

"What more can David say to you? For You know Your servant, O Sovereign Lord. For the sake of Your word and according to Your will, You have done this great thing and made it known to Your servant.

"How great You are, O Sovereign Lord! There is no one like You, and there is no God but You. Your words are trustworthy, and You have promised these good things to Your servant. You, O Sovereign Lord, have spoken, and with Your blessing, the house of Your servant will be blessed forever."

There is no question how much David loved the Lord! But what about you and me? How do we go about loving God with all our hearts, soul, and strength?

Looking at the various scriptures that deal with this subject, Jesus added "mind" to the list. He said, "Love the Lord Your God with all your heart, and with all your soul, and with all your mind and with all your strength." He said this as an answer to a Jewish teacher of the law who promptly replied, "Well said, Teacher. You are right in saying that God is One and there is no other than Him, to love Him with all your heart, with all your understanding, and with all your strength." This teacher of the law left off the word "soul," and the word "understanding" could be a used instead of "mind." He lumped "soul and mind" into the word "heart" (Mark 12:30, 32–33).

How do we go about loving God with
all our hearts, soul, and strength?

7 SECRETS

It sounds more complicated than it really is. The bottom line
is that taken all together, it means we need to love the Lord with
all our emotional strength. "Soul" in the original Hebrew word
means "breath of life" or "that which God breathed into man
at the very beginning." "Spirit" also means "breath" or "wind,"
and, throughout the Old Testament, these words are used inter-
changeably. Most scholars believe we are in two parts: Our spirit,
soul, and mind are all lumped into the word "heart," while our
body, our flesh, is the other part.

That makes it a little easier to understand rather than trying
to figure out how to love Him with all of those things separately
or together. Because God is the One who looks at the heart, we
have to understand that He knows our thoughts, desires, dreams,
emotions, loves, goals. All of it. So He requires that we love Him
with our heart and with all our strength, which means with all
our might, stamina, and energy.

We need to love the Lord with
all our emotional strength.

7 SECRETS

Here are some things David said to express his love to the
Lord:

+ "O God, you are My God. Earnestly I seek You.
My body longs for You in a dry and weary land

where there is no water. Because Your love is
better than life, my lips will glorify You. I will
praise You as long as I live, and in Your name I
will lift up my hands" (Ps. 63:1, 3–4).

+ "I will praise You, O Lord my God, with all my
heart; I will glorify Your name forever" (Ps. 86:12).

+ "I said to the Lord, You are my Lord" (Ps. 16:2).

Then, from that great Psalm 103:1, he says, "Praise the
Lord, O my soul, *all my inmost being*, praise His Holy Name"
(emphasis mine).

Because most of us want to be sure we honor this great commandment, two words pop out that are not talked about that
much. The first is the word "all" our heart, and the other is all
our "strength."

The "all" scripture that often comes to my mind is found
in Revelation 3. The spirit of God is talking to the church at
Laodicea. True, you and I are not a church, but you can quickly
get the idea of how God looks at "all." He says, "I know your
deeds, that you are neither cold nor hot. I wish you were either
one or the other! So, because you are lukewarm, I am about to
spit you out of my mouth."

He goes on and mentions that they are so busy with the
affairs of life, they are distracted from loving God the way He
has intended. So He offers a chance for repentance: "Here I am.
I stand at the door and knock. If anyone hears My voice and
opens the door, I will come in and eat with him and he with Me"
(Rev. 3:15–16, 20).

Inside I have this compelling, driving desire to have my life
and everything I do to totally count for God and make a difference in the world. It has always been there; I can't help it. Even
as a grade-school kid who never went to church, I knew. One
day, some of us fourth- and fifth-graders were playing on the

weekend in the woods in central Michigan. We were tired, so we sat down and went around the circle with the subject, "What do you want to be when you grow up?" The answers were, as you can imagine, all the normal professions like nurse, fireman, policeman, and doctor. Then it was my turn. I blurted out, "I am going to serve God." I was as surprised as they were!

In the ninth grade, I finally made a real commitment to the Lord. From that moment on, I strived to live the Christian life I was being taught. I got involved with Youth for Christ and started a Bible Club at my high school. Many of my friends were finding a relationship with Christ as their Savior, and I was pretty focused on YFC and leading the singing for my youth group at church.

When I went to a Christian college, it became even more important. I had no time to "shoot the bull" over a cup of coffee in the cafeteria. Taking maximum credits (units) per semester while working, I still let nothing get in the way of my morning time with the Lord. My prayer was always the same: "God, please, use me! I'm your man. I'll go wherever you want me to go, and I'll do whatever you ask." And when I read in Ezekiel that God was looking for someone to stand in the gap, I started praying for Him to let me be the one to stand in the gap, whatever that meant. When I read in Isaiah that God said, "Who will go for us?" I answered daily, "Choose me. I will go for You!" Wherever it was, He wanted someone to go.

Minneapolis has a lot of churches, and from time to time, "deeper life" teachers from England would show up in town. I would be there every night, listening and growing. One time, a preacher named Stephen Olford of London came to my college and preached in the chapel. His subject was "Totalitarian Surrender." I was all over that, and I still work on it today.

Over my life, God has blessed me far and above any dreams I could have ever had. Just thinking about it as I write this brings on all the emotions.

All that leads to the "all" reason for this digression. I always thought I was loving God as He wanted until one day a disaster came to my home. It took a dear friend to help me see the real issue.

It was in 1997 and it just about crippled my heart. I spent many days out there on the lava rocks, listening to the ocean, and crying out to the Lord, "Why are you allowing this? Don't you see this situation?" and on and on. Then, one day, I found a book on my shelf by my now-late friend, Keith Miller. Just the title of the book threw me off. So I called him and told him that his book was ruining my life! He said to me, "You get yourself down here to Austin immediately."

I flew to Texas and spent a few days with Keith and his lovely wife, Andrea. Keith and I walked the city, sat in parks, and talked. He told me that we were a lot alike, and he explained how he got past such occasions in his life, much like the one I was going through.

Even all these years later, the one thing he said to me that still rings in my ears almost every day is this. He said, "Let's say you have ten thousand acres." Well, he knew I didn't own even one. He continued, "You have dedicated all of it to the Lord." I totally understood that concept. "But somehow you have kept one acre back. God is trying to get your attention because He wants *all* of it, not just 9,999!"

Now I fully understood, "All!" God wants us to love Him with *all* our hearts, totally, fully, not holding anything back. I constantly search my own heart, as we all should, to make sure we are *all* His.

This reminds me of a song Jamie Owens Collins and Gary Chapman used to sing:

> "I'm Yours, Lord,
> Everything I've got,
> Everything I'm not, I'm Yours, Lord,
> Try me now and see,

See if I can be completely Yours!"
—"I'M YOURS LORD," MUSIC AND LYRICS BY BRENDA LEE

> God wants us to love Him with
> *all* our hearts, totally, fully, not
> holding anything back.

7 SECRETS

He wants all of our hearts, and He wants all of our strength.
Here are a couple of verses to put it into perspective:

+ "Whatever you do, whether in word or deed, do it
  all in the name of the Lord Jesus, giving thanks to
  God the Father through Him" (Paul, Col. 3:17).

+ "Whatever you do, work at it with all your heart, as
  working for the Lord, not for men" (Paul, Col. 3:23).

In 2 Samuel 6, it says that David brought the ark to Jerusalem.
What happened indicates how he loved God with all his strength!
"David, wearing a linen ephod, danced before the Lord with all
his might while he, and the entire house of Israel, brought up the
ark of the Lord with shouts of joy and the sound of the trumpets."
But, as may be the case at some point in our lives, not everyone
was pleased with David's praising and loving the Lord with all his
strength.
"As the ark of the Lord was entering the city of David, Michal,
daughter of Saul, David's wife, watched from a window.
"And, when she saw King David leaping and dancing before
the Lord, she despised him in her heart." When challenged by
her and her disgust, David said, "I will celebrate before the Lord.
I will become even more undignified than this, and I will be
humiliated in my own eyes" (2 Sam. 6:14–16, 21–22).

Loving God with all our strength means that when given the opportunity, we put all we have into the challenge and opportunity, whether at church, or following God's absolute call for our lives, or even as volunteers in the community. Underneath it all, we have made that commitment to stand tall and to love God with all our strength.

David's final words on the subject: "O my Strength, I will sing praise to You. You, O God, are my fortress, my loving God" (Ps. 59:17).

How do you think God feels about a partial commitment? How do you relate to the word "all"?

> Loving God with all our strength means that when given the opportunity, we put all we have into the challenge and opportunity, whether at church, or following God's absolute call for our lives, or even as volunteers in the community.

7 SECRETS

Loving God with all his heart opened David's heart to love his neighbors and all those he served in the same manner as he wanted them to love him in return. He knew the principle that just being there for them would be enough.

Six

BE THERE, LIKE A GOOD NEIGHBOR

DAVID'S SECRET # 6

He Loved His Neighbors, His Family, and His Friends

"Lord…who may live in Your holy hill? He…who speaks the truth…who does his neighbor no wrong, and casts no slur on his fellowman (David, Ps. 15:1–3).

"Do to others what you would have them do to you" (Jesus, Luke 6:31).

"Love your neighbor as yourself" (God, Levit. 19:18; Jesus, Matt. 22:39).

"They will know we are Christians by our love, by our love,
They will know we are Christians by our love.
We will walk with each other, we will walk hand in hand,
We will walk with each other, we will walk hand in hand
And, together, we will spread the news, that God is in our land.
And they'll know we are Christians by our love, by our love.
Yes, they'll know we are Christians by our love."
—"THEY WILL KNOW WE ARE CHRISTIANS BY OUR LOVE," WORDS AND MUSIC BY PETER SCHOLTES

Loving your neighbor as yourself is one of the basic laws God laid down in the very beginning to help men live peaceably with each other. Testing Jesus on this question, an expert in the law asked him, "But who is really my neighbor?" Jesus answered this question with the story of the Good Samaritan. In this story, or parable, a man traveling from Jerusalem to Jericho was robbed, beaten, and left half-dead. Many good people passed by but did nothing. A priest and a Levite (Jewish temple leader), were among those who passed by him.

But a Samaritan, someone from the other side of the tracks, someone who was "less than," stopped and helped him. The Samaritan bandaged his wounds, took him to an inn, paid to have him taken care of, and then left. In this case, Jesus said, the man's neighbor was the Samaritan, the one who had mercy on him.

In the extreme, it would be like a Palestinian giving an Israelite a hand, or an extremist Muslim aiding a Christian who needed help. But a more common example is the guy at the grocery store parking lot with a sign that says, "Hungry, please help, and God bless." Neighbors? We don't often think of them that way, but Jesus did, and so did David.

After David had killed Goliath, Jonathan, the King's son, befriended him. Because David had nothing appropriate for this new life, in a show of friendship, Jonathan gave David his robe, his tunic, his sword, his bow, and even his belt. These two men became best friends. It reminds one of the powerful friendship between Marsala, the Roman Tribune, and Judah Ben-Hur in that great novel by Lew Wallace. David and Jonathan had a lot in common, both had high rank in Saul's army, they were strong valiant leaders, and both were in line to be the next king.

Saul, of course, eventually became angry about Jonathan's friendship with David and yelled at one point, "Don't I know that you have sided with the son of Jesse to your own shame? As long as David lives on this earth, neither you nor your kingdom will be established. Now, bring him to me, for he must die!"

But knowing Samuel's prophecy that his father's kingdom would end and David would be the next king, Jonathan made a covenant with David. He asked that David would not cut off his descendants after he became king, as would have been the normal custom.

Some years later, after David was well established as king, he asked his advisors if any descendants were left from Jonathan. He was told there was a man crippled in both feet who was the son of Jonathan and whose nurse had fallen with him as a child, while they were fleeing from the Philistines, as they had just killed Saul and Jonathan and were taking over the country. His name was Mephibosheth. David sent for him and sat him at the king's table, like one of his own sons, for the rest of his life. Mephibosheth was David's neighbor, and he helped David fulfill a promise he had made to his father, David's friend.

Good neighbor, bad neighbor? I have a friend who had a disgruntled neighbor. This neighbor kept planting things just on my friend's side of the property line, and of course this irritated her, and my friend promptly dug them back up. They quarreled and finally made peace. But before she knew it, there was a new plant or bush growing on her property again! In her case, it seemed to never really end.

The disciple Peter asked Jesus this question in Matthew 18:21: "How many times shall I forgive my brother (neighbor) when he sins against me? Up to seven times?" Jesus answered, "I tell you, not seven times, but seventy-seven times."

What about a friend, a good friend, who turns against you? How do you keep loving such a person after such a big hurt, especially when that person continues to hurt you? We have all had this happen to some degree, and every situation may have to be handled differently. But Proverbs 10:12 says, "Love covers over all wrongs." We are told again and again in scripture to love one another. Bill Bright, the founder of Campus Crusade, once said, "The only way to love some people is to love them by faith." Whatever works!

> How do you keep loving such a person
> after such a big hurt, especially when
> that person continues to hurt you?

7 SECRETS

David wrote as a young man in a dramatic way, "If I have done evil to him who is at peace with me, or without cause have robbed my foe, then let my enemy pursue and overtake me. Let him trample my life to the ground and make me sleep in the dust!" (Ps. 7:4–5).

Friendship was a serious thing to David. He loved his men and called them his brothers, and they, in return, said things like this in Chronicles 12:18: "We are yours, O David. We are with you, O son of Jesse. Success, success to you and success to those who help you, for your God will help you."

Later, in his fifties, David was once again fighting a giant. This one was the same size as Goliath, also a descendant of Rapha. His name was Ishbi-Benob. David fought him but became exhausted. He was rescued by one of his mighty men, Abishai who killed the giant. You could say he had a great relationship with his army throughout his life, a true Band of Brothers!

After he had united all of Israel after seven years of civil war, winning the love and support of both sides, here is what was said of David in 2 Samuel 3:36: "All the people took note and were pleased; indeed, everything the King did pleased them." Wow! What a testimony about someone who did not take advantage of position but showed love and concern to all of those around him. It is true that when a man's ways please the Lord, even his enemies are at peace with him.

Many years later, as David was escaping Jerusalem from his son, Absalom, on his way toward Jericho, a man named Shimei from the same clan as Saul ran along beside the road and threw stones at David and cursed him. Of course, one of David's men asked permission to cut off his head. But, David allowed Shimei to curse him. David said to his men, "My son, who is of my own flesh, is trying to take my life; how much more, then, this Benjaminite. Leave him alone."

Then after the battle, when David was on his way back to Jerusalem, Shimei showed up again. This time, falling prostrate on his face, he asked for forgiveness, and David promised that he would not die. David's interest was not revenge, but to bind together a nation in distress as peacefully as possible. Shimei did not act neighborly, but David, in return, treated him with kindness.

But I am getting ahead of the story here, and lest you think David never had a neighbor, friend, or family member who betrayed him, think again.

ABSALOM

Absalom was David's third son. His mother, Maacah, was a princess, daughter of the King of Geshur. Surely this union was to keep peace between the two kings.

The description of the young man (prince), Absalom, is astonishing. "In all Israel, there was not a man so highly praised for his handsome appearance as Absalom. From the top of his head to the sole of his foot, there was no blemish in him. Whenever he cut the hair of his head—he used to cut his hair from time to time when it became too heavy for him—he would weigh it, and its weight was two hundred shekels by the royal standard (five pounds)" (2 Sam. 14:25–26). Here was the beginning of what would be known in my generation as "big hair."

He had a blustery, young manhood. Once, acting in revenge,

he killed his half-brother, Amnon, who had raped his sister, Tamar. Because of that, he was banished from the kingdom and fled to Geshur. Eventually, David forgave him and welcomed him back to the royal family.

ABSALOM'S CONSPIRACY (2 SAM. 15–18)

Absalom had a high opinion of himself. As the king's son, he provided himself with a chariot, horses, and fifty men to run ahead of him. His custom was to sit at the city gate early every morning, greet all the people with a handshake and a kiss, and solve their complaints and problems so they did not have to bother King David for justice. In this way, he stole the hearts of the people.

After four years, Absalom made his move. He gained permission from the king to offer sacrifices in Hebron. But he sent secret messengers all over Israel to say, "As soon as you hear the sound of the trumpets, then say, 'Absalom is King in Hebron.'" The conspiracy had gained strength, and Absalom's followers kept on increasing.

David's closest friend and advisor was Ahithophel. It was said of him, "Now in those days, the advice Ahithophel gave was like that of one who inquires of God." That was how both David and Absalom regarded all of Ahithophel's advice. He had been both friend and advisor to David throughout his reign as king. Then Ahithophel went over to Absalom! David's response was immediate. "Come! We must flee, or none of us will escape from Absalom."

David remembered Nathan's pronouncement from God after the Bathsheba incident that one from his own household would bring disaster down upon him. This was it! A son and his best friend, he was betrayed! How could it be worse than that? It couldn't. In deep distress he wrote, "If an enemy were insulting me, I could endure it. If a foe were raising himself against me, I could hide from him. But it is you, a man like myself, my companion, my close friend, with whom I once enjoyed sweet fellowship as we walked with the throng at the house of God. My companion attacks his friends; he violates his covenant. His speech is smooth as butter, yet war is in his heart."

So how did David handle this disaster, which was happening to him near the end of his great career? In the next series of verses, we have the answer. David said, "Cast your cares on the Lord, and He will sustain you; He will never let the righteous fall. As for me, I trust in you." David trusted that the Lord would absolutely deliver him. Earlier in the same psalm, he asks the Lord to "confuse the wicked, and confound their speech" (Ps. 55:9, 12, 14, 20–23). And that is exactly what happened next.

As he was leaving Jerusalem in disgrace and climbing up the Mount of Olives with his large entourage, David prayed a prayer that was simple but to the point: "O Lord, turn Ahithophel's counsel into foolishness."

> David trusted that the Lord
> would absolutely deliver him.

7 SECRETS

When David arrived at the summit, Hushai, the Arkite, also a counselor and friend, was there to greet him, his robe torn and dust on his head. David asked him to return to Jerusalem and pledge allegiance to the new king, Absalom, and say, "I will be your servant, O King; I was your father's servant in the past, but now I will be your servant" (2 Sam. 15:31, 34).

Hushai was asked to be a spy in the new kingdom, most likely at great risk to himself. David had also sent his priest, Zadok, and his son Abiathar, back to Jerusalem. He instructed them to send their two sons, Ahimaaz and Jonathan, to him with any information they heard from Absalom—two more young spies.

Hushai had just arrived as Absalom was entering the city. On taking the city, Absalom asked Ahithophel for his advice. Ahithophel said to Absalom, "'I would choose twelve thousand men and set out tonight in pursuit of David. I would attack him while he is weary and weak. I would strike down only the king and bring all the people back to you.' This plan seemed good to Absalom and all the elders of Israel. But Absalom said, 'Summon also Hushai' [who had already pledged allegiance to the new king], so we can hear what he has to say.'"

When asked, Hushai responded, "The advice Ahithophel has given is not good this time. You know your father and his men. They are fighters and as fierce as a wild bear robbed of her cubs. Besides, your father is an experienced fighter; he will not spend the night with the troops. Even now, he is hidden in a cave or some other place. So I advise you, let all Israel, as numerous as the sand on the seashore be gathered to you, with you yourself leading them into battle. Neither he nor any of his men will be left alive."

Absalom and all the men of Israel said, "The advice of Hushai is better than that of Ahithophel" (2 Sam. 17:7–9, 11–12, 14).

Then Hushai sent the two boys, sons of the priests, with all this information to David with an urgent message to cross the Jordan River at once because Ahithophel has advised such and such. So David and all those with him, set out and crossed the Jordan that night.

In the meantime, when Ahithophel saw that his advice had not been followed, he went to his hometown, put his house in order, and hanged himself! God had frustrated the advice of Ahithophel to bring disaster upon Absalom.

David had many friends, real neighbors, on the other side of the Jordan River. They brought all kinds of provisions for his family and his growing army. Then thousands, faithful to the king, came to him from all over Israel. Finally came the day when the battle with the forces of Absalom was set. The commanders would not let David join the battle because his life was too precious. David pleaded with them to be gentle with the young man Absalom, for his sake. Even then, David was thinking of his son. What a dilemma.

Twenty thousand men died that day, and the battle was spread over the whole countryside. A historian said the forest claimed more lives that day than the sword. One of those in the forest was Absalom. He was fleeing from David's men, riding his mule. When the mule went under the thick branches of an oak tree, his head and hair got caught in the tree, while his mule kept on going and left him hanging in midair.

General Joab put three javelins through Absalom's heart, and he died in that tree. He was then thrown into a pit in the forest, where they piled a large heap of rocks over him. The trumpets sounded, and the war was over.

When David was told what happened, his only concern was for Absalom. He went up to his room and wept. "O my son, Absalom! My son, my son, Absalom! If only I had died instead of you. O Absalom, my son, my son!" (2 Sam. 18:33). The grief of a father who has lost a child he loved, even given these terrible circumstances, is more than he could bear. David loved his son in spite of his rebellion as he loved all his family, his neighbors, his friends, and those who followed his leadership.

Love Your Neighbor as Yourself

How can we do this? For one thing, we need to read a lot of scriptures that talk about how we are to treat our brothers, our neighbors, and people in general. We ask the basic question because of our fast-paced lives in the twenty-first century. We are supposed to be patient with the driver in front of us who is driving 35 mph in a 50-mph zone and the guy at the back of us whose vehicle is six inches from our bumper. Or how about the guy in the pickup who just cut you off on the freeway on your way to Costco, where you thought you had a parking space up front before the man in front of you grabbed it? It's no better at the local Walmart or grocery store, either. Lots of people, in a hurry, pay little or no attention to very much around them, but obviously are stressed and not in a neighborly mood.

You think it's easier in poorer countries, other cities around the world, like Nairobi or Kathmandu, with too many cars everywhere, coming at you in every direction with no distinct lanes, horns blaring and exhaust fumes choking you to death? "Live peaceably with all men," the Bible says. But how? "Judge not!" It seems impossible.

I believe that once David was at home in Jerusalem, life was easier. Because of his huge capacity for integrity, he found a way to be fair and just and to truly love his family, friends, and neighbors. I have found only verses and stories that show him as generous, forgiving, and honest in his thinking and dealings. However, the one documented time he did hurt a friend, the consequences were overwhelming, as we saw in an earlier chapter.

The apostle Paul, in Romans 12, helps us with this issue. These are verses we know, like verse 3: "Do not think of yourself more highly than you ought." And verse 10: "Be devoted to one another in brotherly love; honor one another above yourselves." And verse 13: "Share with God's people who are in need. Practice hospitality." And finally, verse 18: "If it is possible, as far as it depends on you, live at peace with everyone."

Those are some things we can really work on if we want to love our neighbors as ourselves. The thing is, we really need to do this because very big things are at stake.

"Go into all the world and preach the good news to all creation" (Jesus, Mark 16:15). There is no way to follow that command without neighborly love, a desire to want to help people, and thinking of them above ourselves.

I am reminded of a sadly hilarious sketch The Jeremiah People used to do in the '70s and '80s called "The Park Bench." In this sketch, an average man was sitting in the middle of a park bench, eating a banana, when two young men walked up, discussing different ways to share the "Good News." Two seats were available, one on each side of this man. They continued with their discussion. It got heated, and then we heard phrases like "the four spiritual laws," "the bridge," "evangelism explosion," "the button-hole approach," "tracts," "preaching on street corners," on and on, along with names of major preachers and evangelists.

The unsuspecting man in the middle listened and looked back and forth at each man, again and again, during the argument as each gave his heated opinion. Suddenly, tempers boiling over, one of them smacked his hands together so loudly that the man in the middle jumped and gasped, and down went the whole banana! The man was choking! He got a quick pat on the back until the banana went down. Finally, when he was OK and everything settled down, he calmly said to his park-bench buddies, "Hey, guys, I'd like to hear more about that good news you have been talking about." The two Christian men glanced at their watches, jumped up, made excuses, and quickly left!

The thing is, whether we are part of a church, a parachurch organization, or just an average working person in one of thousands of different vocations, professional and not, we all have the same charge, the same responsibility. Loving our neighbors opens the doors to share all kinds of things with others, especially The Good News.

Jesus said, "For God so loved the world that He gave his one and only Son, that whoever believes in Him shall not perish but have eternal life" (John 3:16).

Paul said to young Timothy, "The Lord's servant...must be kind to everyone...gently instruct, in the hope that God will grant them repentance leading them to a knowledge of the truth!" (2 Tim. 2:24–25).

"How good and pleasant it is when brothers live together in unity. It is like precious oil poured on the head" (David, Ps. 133:1–2).

> Loving our neighbors opens the doors
> to share all kinds of things with
> others, especially The Good News.

7 SECRETS

What could be the result of your being a "good neighbor" to someone with different beliefs and values than your own?

David, Paul, and Jesus all believed we could love our neighbor as ourselves and love God with all our heart and strength. When we live in this way, a heart of worship is one of the best results. David worshipped the Lord in every situation, sometimes quietly and sometimes *loudly.*

Seven

CRY OUT AND SHOUT

DAVID'S SECRET #7

He Had a Heart of Worship

"The whole crowd of disciples began joyfully to Praise God in loud voices.... Some of the Pharisees in the crowd said to Jesus, 'Teacher, rebuke your disciples.' 'I tell you,' He replied, 'If they keep quiet, the stones will cry out'" (Luke 19:37, 39–40).

"Clap your hands, all you nations; *shout* to God with *cries* of joy. How awesome is the Lord Most High, the great King over all the earth" (emphasis mine, The Sons of Korah, Ps. 47:1–2).

"Ascribe to the Lord the glory due His name; *worship the Lord* in the splendor of His holiness" (emphasis mine, David, Ps. 29:2).

"Yet a time is coming, and has now come, when the true worshippers will worship the Father in spirit and truth, for they are the kind of worshippers the Father seeks. God is a spirit, and His worshippers must worship in spirit and in truth" (Jesus, John 4:23–24).

"O Lord my God, when I in awesome wonder
Consider all the worlds thy hands have made.
I see the stars, I hear the rolling thunder,

Thy power throughout the universe displayed:
Then sings my soul, my savior God to thee:
How great thou art! How great thou art!
Then sings my soul, my savior God to thee:
How great thou art! How great thou art!"
—"HOW GREAT THOU ART," WORDS AND MUSIC
BY STUART K. HINE (OLD SWEDISH MELODY)

T WAS THE greatest praise gathering ever recorded. All of Israel had come together in Jerusalem to celebrate the building of the temple for the *name* of the Lord and the final anointing of David's son, Solomon, as the next king.

David charged all the leaders of Israel to help Solomon build the temple. He said, "Now devote your heart and soul to seeking the Lord your God. Begin to build the sanctuary of the Lord so that you may bring the ark of the Covenant of the Lord and the sacred articles belonging to God into the temple that will be built for the name of the Lord" (1 Chron. 22:19).

A few years earlier, the ark of God was brought to Jerusalem with great celebration. This was the one Moses had made hundreds of years before that contained two stone tablets inscribed with the Ten Commandments. This new temple was to house the Ark of the Covenant of God.

David ordered worship before the ark when he had assembled all of Israel in Jerusalem. First, he appointed 818 descendants of Aaron and the Levites to lead the worship before the Ark.

Then he told these leaders to appoint their brothers as singers to sing joyful songs, accompanied by musical instruments such as lyres, flutes, trumpets, harps, and cymbals. Kenaniah, the head Levite, was appointed as their director in charge of the singing. 1 Chronicles 15:22 says, "It was his responsibility because he was skillful at it." I love that! A total of 288 were selected because they were skilled in music.

So here came the ark. All the singers were clothed in robes of fine linen, as was David and all the Levites, dancing and praising before the Lord. He could have written Psalm 68 for such an occasion. Here are his words from verse 24: "Your procession has come into view, O God, the procession of my God and King into the sanctuary. In front are the singers, after them the musicians; with them are the maidens playing tambourines. Sing to God, O kingdoms of the earth, sing praise to the Lord, to Him who rides the ancient skies above, who thunders with mighty voice. Proclaim the power of God whose Majesty is over Israel, whose power is in the skies. You are awesome, O God, in your sanctuary. Praise be to God" (Ps. 68:24–25, 32–35).

Then, at the much larger worship event, David anointed his son, Solomon, to be king and announced the building of the temple in Jerusalem. David had appointed four thousand of the Levite descendants to praise the Lord with musical instruments he provided for this event. All of these musicians, along with unnumbered singers, all the elders of Israel, all the commanders of thousand and hundreds (twelve divisions of 24,000 men), officers of the twelve tribes of Israel, along with all the priests, gatekeepers, the king's overseers and family, and people from every village and town from all over Israel gathered in Jerusalem, celebrating both the news of the new temple to be built and Solomon's anointing as the new king.

What a praise and worship event! David praised the Lord in the presence of the whole assembly (at least three hundred thousand strong) saying, (loudly, I am sure, and with his hands raised to heaven and his voice in the same direction), "Praise be to You, O Lord, God of our father Israel, from everlasting to everlasting. Yours, O Lord, is the greatness and the power and the glory and the majesty and the splendor. For everything in heaven and earth is Yours.

"Yours, O Lord, is the kingdom. You are exalted as head over all. Wealth and honor come from You. You are the ruler of all things. In Your hands are strength and power to exalt and give strength to all. Now, our God, we give You thanks and praise Your glorious name.

"Then David said to the whole assembly, 'Praise the Lord Your God.' So they all praised the Lord, the God of their fathers; they bowed low and fell prostrate before the Lord and the king."

It was amazing! And certainly not a quiet worship experience on that day.

"The next day, they made sacrifices to the Lord and presented burnt offerings to Him, a thousand bulls, a thousand rams, a thousand male lambs, together with their drink offerings, and other sacrifices in abundance for all Israel. They ate and drank with great joy in the presence of the Lord all day."

"Then they acknowledged Solomon, son of David, as King" (1 Chron. 29:10–13, 20–23).

There is no doubt that David's heart, his words, and his songs are what the Christian world has always looked to as the ultimate teacher of worship. Out of the 150 psalms, David is recognized as having written 74 of them and possibly more that scholars have not identified during the past three thousand years. In addition to the great hymn writers of the past few hundred years, contemporary worship and praise songwriters have been writing music to David's words as well. Most notably, in the '60s and '70s, David and Dale Garrett of Scripture and Song from New Zealand put together many song books. Many others have come onto the scene in recent years, including today's top songwriters like Chris Tomlin, Matt Redman, Michael W. Smith, and so many others.

> There is no doubt that David's heart,
> his words, and his songs are what the
> Christian world has always looked to
> as the ultimate teacher of worship.

7 SECRETS

When Michael W. Smith wrote "Great Is the Lord," it became his first recorded praise and worship song. "Last on the Michael W. Smith Rock and Pop Project Album, just a song in 6/8 time...a little thing plus a choir," he says. Debbie, his wife, wrote down the lyrics from various Psalms right out of the scripture, and he would put them to music. When you look at David's Psalm 145:3, you can see where she got the title "Great Is the Lord and Most Worthy of Praise." Michael says, "I've sung that one a whole lot of times!"

David had no great church buildings or cathedrals in which to present his songs of worship, but as he said in Psalm 9, "I will praise You, O Lord, with all my *heart*; I will tell of all Your wonders. I will be glad and rejoice in You; I will sing praise to Your name, O Most High" (emphasis mine, Ps. 9:1–2). He had a heart of worship all the time. It was his cathedral for praise.

David wore his praise on his sleeve! Everyone knew how he felt about the Lord. He wrote about what God was doing for him after a particularly difficult time. "He put a new song in my mouth, a hymn of praise to our God. Many will see and fear and put their trust in the Lord. I proclaim righteousness in the great assembly; I do not seal my lips, as You know, O Lord. I speak of Your faithfulness and salvation. I do not conceal Your love and Your truth from the great assembly..." (Ps. 40:3, 9–10).

David was called Israel's Singer of Songs, and along with all the songs and lyrics he wrote and sang, we know he played many instruments. "I will sing a new song to You, O God," he says in

Psalm 144. "On the ten stringed lyre I will make music to You."
No wonder he was emotional and such a charismatic leader. He
was an artist! Not many warriors, or conquering kings, had also
been shepherds and musicians.

Many of David's songs were to be accompanied by the instruments of the day—harps, lutes, flutes, trumpets, and cymbals,
just to name a few. They were built on the themes of his life and
of the day and age in which he lived. They were about joy, praise,
pain, prayer, sorrow, glory, relationship, virtues, anger, worship, good and bad people, majesty and glory of God, heartache,
thankfulness, success, failure, happiness, mournfulness, troubles, enemies, friends, and story songs of hate and love. Doesn't
that sound like our country music themes of today? Jerusalem,
because of David, was the Nashville of 1,000 BC!

> David wore his praise on his sleeve!
> Everyone knew how he felt about the Lord.

7 SECRETS

Today, in many contemporary churches, worship is the first
part of a service, with lyrics on the screen, a band on the stage,
and a leader singing the melody so we can all join in. This is the
type of worship time many Christians experience on Sunday
mornings. And although many people are worshipping the Lord
during this time, many are not, as well. Real worship is a matter
of the heart, where love, devotion, and respect are shown to God,
our Creator, and His Son, Jesus Christ, our Savior. In most cases,
the style of the music is bringing people into a wonderful worship experience. In other cases, the music performance may actually take someone emotionally away from an attitude of worship.
It is an extremely personal thing.

Having grown up in the early years of Christian music with

a Sunday-morning hymn or two, a song by the choir, plus some special music, usually by a soloist, it was hard for me to get used to today's worship bands before the morning sermon to get me into a worshipful attitude. Yet, I can promise you, in other Christian musical settings, the drums and instruments, along with twenty great singers, choreography, lights, and sound, were totally OK! The changes have been significant, but real worship is the central issue.

Fearing that his music had taken the place of what God really wants in his worshipers, Matt Redman penned this song:

> When the music fades,
> And all is stripped away,
> And I simply come,
> Longing just to bring
> Something that's of worth
> That will bless your heart.
>
> I'll bring you more than a song,
> For a song in itself
> Is not what you have required.
> You search much deeper within
> Through the way things appear,
> You're looking into my heart.
>
> I'm coming back to the heart of worship
> And it's all about You, it's all about You, Jesus.
> I'm sorry, Lord, for the thing I've made it
> When it's all about You, it's all about you, Jesus.
> —"HEART OF WORSHIP," WORDS AND
> MUSIC BY MATT REDMAN

There is no question that David had a heart of worship. Just read these words of his from Psalm 86:12: "I will praise You, O

Lord, my God, with all my heart; I will glorify Your name forever." It's not that David was in an attitude of worship in his mind every minute of every day. There was also a country to govern, people's issues to judge, wars and battles to fight and win, and various circumstances to overcome. We are the same. Yet, no matter our difficulties or successes, we can still have a heart of worship. It is always there, and when it is, no matter what you do throughout your day, or what circumstances you face, you will be reminded from time to time of the love you have for the Lord. Underneath it all, you can have a heart of gratefulness and worship.

Have you ever been to a service and felt that during the music worship segment, some people were displaying their worship just so that others would notice how spiritual they were? It is not for you or me to judge because it is God, and only God, who looks into someone's heart. But you can't fake out the Lord, and true worship is serious business.

Such seriousness is exemplified in a story that occurred during the end of David's reign. It could have been placed in the chapter on prayer because prayer turned the circumstance around. Or maybe forgiveness, because after admitting his wrongdoing, what happened next is our story. Or it could have been under the virtues because of David's generosity and his integrity in dealing with the solution. But it is here, under "worship," because of the ultimate necessity that we are to understand and be serious about our worship actions and their final results.

ARAUNAH'S THRESHING FLOOR
(1 CHRON. 21 AND 22:1)

Near the end of David's kingship, historians tell us that he rested from conquering all his neighbor lands and finally had peace. On one occasion, he just wanted to know how many able, fighting men he really had in his kingdom, just in case.

The thing is, God never allowed the Israelites to even have horses for their battles because God wanted them to know He was fighting for them. It's the same here. It's not how big the army could be, but how much David depended on the Lord so that he could realize that all he had accomplished was not just because he was a great leader or powerful warrior. God had to get the glory. That's just how it was, and really, how He wants it to be in our lives today as well. Not that we shouldn't look at our own circumstances and use the intelligence and free will God gave us to at least do our part.

So David ordered Joab, his general, and his commanders, to go throughout the land and count the able, fighting men. Joab tried his best to dissuade the king, to no avail. So they went east, then north, then west, then south and covered every village and town in all of Israel. Nine and a half months later, they reported to David that there were more than one and a half million able men who could draw the sword. Wow! That's a big army in a day when conscription was absolute, should it be necessary. The day this report was given to David, he was conscience-stricken and immediately prayed, "I have sinned greatly by doing this. Now, I beg You, take away the guilt of Your servant. I have done a very foolish thing." Ahh, the weight of it. You can feel it! And there came Gad, the prophet, with a word from the Lord, the consequence!

"So Gad went to David and said to him, 'This is what the Lord says; take your choice. Three years of famine, three months of being swept away before your enemies with their swords overtaking you or three days of the sword of the Lord, days of plague in the land, with the angel of the Lord ravaging every part of Israel. Now, then, decide how I should answer the One who sent me.'

"David said to Gad, 'I am in deep distress. Let me fall into the hands of the Lord, for His mercy is very great, but do not let me fall into the hands of men.'

"So the Lord sent a plague on Israel, and seventy thousand men fell dead. And God sent an angel to destroy Jerusalem, but as the angel was doing so, the Lord saw it and was grieved. 'Enough! Withdraw your hand.' David looked up and saw the angel of the Lord standing between heaven and earth with a drawn sword in his hand extended over Jerusalem. Then, David and the elders of Israel, clothed in sackcloth, fell face down, and David prayed, 'I am the one who has sinned and has done wrong, these are but sheep.... O Lord, my God, let your hand fall upon me and my family, but do not let this plague remain on Your people.'

"Then the angel of the Lord ordered Gad to tell David to go up and build an altar to the Lord on the threshing floor of Araunah the Jebusite. So David went up in obedience. While Araunah was threshing his wheat, he turned and saw the angel, and his four sons hid themselves."

Araunah had to be thinking, *What kind of a day is this!*

"He left his threshing floor and bowed down before David with his face to the ground.

"David said to him, 'Let me have the site of your threshing floor so I can build an altar to the Lord, that the plague on the people may be stopped.'

"'Take it,' Araunah said to David. 'I will give the oxen for the burnt offerings, the threshing sledges for the wood, and the wheat for the grain offerings. I will give all this.'

"'No, I insist on paying the full price,' David replied. 'I will not take for the Lord what is yours, or sacrifice a burnt offering that costs me nothing.'

"So David paid Araunah six hundred shekels of gold for the site [about fifteen pounds, worth about $450,000 today]. David built an altar there to the Lord and sacrificed burnt offerings, fellowship offerings. He called on the Lord, and the Lord answered him with fire from heaven on the altar of burnt offerings."

Years later, Elijah would do the same in a similar sacrifice to prove the power of God over the forces of Baal. In both instances, the fire of the Lord came down in a display of power from heaven and burned up the offerings (1 Chron. 21:8, 11–18, 20–26). Whew! Now there was an immediate answer to prayer to behold!

When David saw that the angel had put away his sword and that the Lord had answered his prayer, he said, "The house of the Lord God is to be built here" (1 Chron. 22:1).

At the beginning of this chapter, we were at the great worship celebration of Solomon's anointing to be king and the announcement for the building of this temple to the name of the Lord. Now we learn it was to be built on the site of Araunah's threshing floor.

Today, if you go to Jerusalem or see a picture of the city, you will see the golden, rounded Dome of the Rock on the city skyline, the awesome current Muslim temple in the center of the city, and below it the remains of the great temple that Solomon built. Below that is the former threshing floor of Araunah the Jebusite.

The center of worship during David's time was in Jerusalem. "I rejoiced with those who said to me, 'Let us go to the house of the Lord. Our feet are standing in Your gates, O Jerusalem. That is where the tribes go up; to praise the name of the Lord'" (Ps. 122:1–2, 4).

A thousand years later, Jesus was discussing worship with a Samaritan woman beside Jacob's well in a city of Samaria. She said, "Our fathers worshipped on this mountain. But you Jews claim that the place we must worship is in Jerusalem."

The center of worship during
David's time was in Jerusalem.

7 SECRETS

Jesus declared, "Believe me, woman, a time is coming when you will worship the Father, neither on this mountain nor in Jerusalem. Yet a time is coming, and has now come, when the true worshippers will worship the Father, in spirit and truth, for they are the kind of worshippers the Father seeks. God is a spirit, and His worshippers must worship in spirit and in truth" (John 4:20–24).

True worship then takes place in our spirits, in our hearts. The place, the music, the occasion, and the time make no difference at all. It doesn't matter whether you are in a magnificent cathedral somewhere in Europe, with ornate art, carvings, and forever-high ceilings with candles lit at the front and sides, just inviting reverence and a worshipful feel, or if you are in a small wooden building on the corner of some little town in America, with a basic pulpit at the front of a few pews where people can kneel to bare their hearts to a loving Savior.

You can also have a great worship experience just standing on a rocky lava ledge with the ocean pounding below, or sitting in a quiet forest somewhere in Colorado in October, with the leaves all in yellow and red, watching them fall to the ground as a mild wind loosens them from a fall branch, or walking a trail through the grandeur of the Rockies anytime, or even more awesome, the great hall of 27,000-foot peaks on both sides while on a trek in the Himalayas. Or better yet, standing on a summit somewhere, anywhere, with nothing but God's greatness in every direction, as you search out other peaks, forests, and views in the distance.

David knew those feelings, too. He said, "The heavens declare the glory of God; the skies proclaim the work of His hands. Day after day, they pour forth in speech; night after night, they display knowledge. There is no speech or language where their voice is not heard. Their voice goes out into all the earth, their words to the ends of the world" (Ps. 19:1–4).

Then, drawing from his *heart of worship*, he says, "Your love, O Lord, reaches to the heavens, Your faithfulness to the skies. Your righteousness is like the mighty mountains, Your justice like the great deep" (Ps. 36:5–6).

Is your worship style quiet and introspective or joyfully loud and expressive? When do you most feel like worshipping the Lord?

The pages in this book have explored what God saw in David's heart. All that remains now is for you to make the commitment to begin your own journey to become a person after God's own heart. You can make these seven secrets, these seven characteristics that David modeled in his life a part of your life, too. The eyes of the Lord still roam the earth, and He is looking to see the changes you will make in your heart.

Eight

YOU CAN DO THIS!

Become a Person After God's Own Heart

IF THIS IS your desire, you can begin to become that person this very day. So you are not overwhelmed, remember the apostle Paul's attitude near the end of his incredible ministry of establishing churches all over his part of the world: "I want to know Christ and the power of His resurrection and the fellowship of sharing in His sufferings, becoming like Him in death, and so, somehow, to attain to the resurrection from the dead. Not that I have already obtained all this, or have already been made perfect, but I press on to take hold of that for which Christ Jesus took hold of for me. Brothers, I do not consider myself yet to have taken hold of it. But one thing I do, forgetting what is behind and straining toward what is ahead, I press on toward the goal to win the prize for which God has called me heavenward in Christ Jesus" (Phil. 3:10–14).

Here, the great apostle Paul admits he is still working on becoming like Christ. And it is OK for you as a Christian to admit that you have not arrived to the point of becoming a person after God's heart yet, either. But the big question is, like Paul, are you prepared to press on and strain toward what is ahead to reach that ultimate goal?

The New Testament teaches us that the Holy Spirit continues working in our hearts even as believers because God is looking for changes in behavior and motives throughout the rest of our lives. The eyes of the Lord are still looking for your committed heart. The apostle Paul said it this way: "Therefore I urge you, brothers, in view of God's mercy, to offer your bodies as living sacrifices, holy and pleasing to God—this is our spiritual act of worship. Do not conform any longer to the pattern of this world, but be transformed by the renewing of your mind. Then you will be able to test and approve what God's will is..." (Rom. 12:1–2).

> And it is OK for you as a Christian to admit that you have not arrived to the point of becoming a person after God's heart yet.

7 SECRETS

After giving the offerings for the new temple Solomon was to build for the name of the Lord, David said these words: "I know my God, that You test the heart and are pleased with integrity...." In the Living Bible, it reads, "I know my God, that you test men to see if they are good; for you enjoy good men" (1 Chron. 29:17).

God created us to worship and praise Him and to give Him pleasure. Working on the characteristics, the "secrets" of becoming a person after God's heart, will certainly give Him great joy and pleasure.

Now, are you ready to "press on to reach that ultimate goal"? If so, then here are some practical things you can do as you begin your journey.

1. First, to be successful, you have to really want to make this a goal. No "almost" attitude is allowed. You have to make a total committed decision to open your heart to becoming all that God wants you to be. You have to put the Lord on the throne in your heart. See Him there. Talk to Him there. Seek to make His attitude your attitude, like the apostle Paul says so many times

and in so many ways all through his epistles. Read
Philippians 2:5–13.

2. Begin to do everything you feel the Lord is asking
   you to do. Face your giants, and ask for God's direction and guidance every day, throughout the day. Ask
   Him to make it clear to you. The amazing thing is,
   He wants it for you more than you do for yourself! So
   you can be sure that if you ask Him to guide you into
   becoming a person after His own heart, then you can
   know for sure you are asking for something that is
   within His will. Jesus said, "You may ask for anything
   in my name, and I will do it." Ask, in Jesus' name every
   time! (John 14:14)

3. Make sure your word is good. Be a person of integrity.
   If you see yourself failing in this area, do your best to
   fix it. Consider how you stand with the list of virtues:
   courage, justice, loyalty, honesty, humility, perseverance,
   patience, faith, trust, and generosity.

4. Strive to be a forgiving person. Remember the principle Jesus laid down: "If you forgive, you will be forgiven" (Luke 6:37). As hard as it might be in certain
   situations where you have been deeply offended and
   hurt, it has to end in forgiveness. There is no other
   option. Don't be stopped in your commitment here,
   even if you make a bad decision or don't act a certain
   way or don't do something you know you should. Pray
   and ask for forgiveness for yourself. Accept the forgiveness, make the change, and move on.

5. Tell the Lord you love Him. Sing a little chorus like
   "I Love You, Lord" or "In Moments Like These." Or
   just think it. This is a big deal. It is the greatest of
   all commandments and cannot be sloughed off. To
   convince the Lord, and yourself, do something that

proves it. Start by telling someone just how much you
love the Lord. That is a good testimony and a great
out-loud confession with your mouth. Do this all the
time to different people. Work at it. Put your heart
into it. That's what the "strength" part of God's command means. It is not a time to be timid. It is not
about standing on the street corner with a sign that
says, "Repent or Go to Hell." It's about being real,
standing strong for what you believe, and talking about
it. You could consider just telling people how much
you love the Lord at church. Give that testimony out
loud, when it is appropriate. In that setting, everyone
is pulling for you, agreeing with you, and praising the
Lord with you.

6. Be a good neighbor! Do your part in a friendly, generous way. This Golden Rule doesn't get you into
God's presence, but it makes living with people so
much easier, and it is not an "ask" from the Lord; it is a
requirement. Learn to love people and act like you love
them. C. S. Lewis said, "If you do that, eventually, you
really will love them"! If someone difficult is in your
life and it seems impossible, ask God to help you love
them by faith.

7. When you are doing all these things, worshipping the
Lord will come so naturally, you won't believe it. It
will happen wherever you are and whenever you think
about it. It won't be a secret. It will be totally apparent,
both to you and those who are with you. You don't
have to be in a worship service at church to worship
the Lord. On the other hand, a church worship time is
one of the most logical and easiest places to do so.

God created us to worship and praise
Him and to give Him pleasure. Working
on the characteristics, the "secrets" of
becoming a person after God's heart, will
certainly give Him great joy and pleasure.

7 SECRETS

All of these practical suggestions involve talking to the Lord and listening for His answers. Open your heart and mind to what you are reading in His word and what you feel you are hearing from Him. Go somewhere often, where you are all alone, where you are able to see, feel, and experience God's majestic creation. Look up at night! Go to a quiet park that has flowers. Take a long walk or a bike ride. If you can, go to the sea, or a lake, or go deep into the woods beside a river or stream. Climb a hill or a mountain, and look out at His marvelous works! Experience quiet! Be grateful for what the Lord is doing in your life, and tell Him that you are thankful. God loves to hear our worship. It's emotional, too, as you will discover.

My prayer for you, and anyone else who takes these thoughts seriously, is that you will get to know the overwhelming feeling of excitement, knowing that you are on the greatest adventure possible for a human being—becoming a person after God's own heart.

Go somewhere often, where you are all
alone, where you are able to see, feel, and
experience God's majestic creation.

7 SECRETS

CHRONOLOGY OF
EVENTS IN DAVID'S LIFE

14–17: Anointed by Samuel

David was most likely anointed by Samuel between 14 and 17, still a teenager.

17–23: In Saul's service

David served Saul for six years. After David had been in Saul's service for some years, 1 Samuel 17:15 says, "But David went back and forth from Saul to tend his father's sheep at Bethlehem," which suggests he started at age seventeen or so.

19–21: Confronting Goliath

The Goliath incident happened sometime during these six years, most likely between 19 and 21. Just after killing Goliath, 1 Samuel 18:2 says that from then on, Saul did not let David return to his father's house. He was given a high rank in the army and was very successful.

23–30: On the run from Saul, banished from the kingdom, building an army

David would have been around twenty-three when he was banished from Saul's household. Many scholars guess that David was on the run from Saul for about seven years, hiding in caves and various cities, subsequently growing a band of raiders that eventually became known as David's Mighty Men. During the last part of this time, he lived in a Philistine City, Ziglag, for a year and four months (1 Sam. 27:7) before the Philistines killed Saul and Jonathan on Mt. Gilboa.

30–37: King in Judah

David was anointed king over Judah when he was thirty years old and reigned in Hebron for seven and a half years.

37–70: King in Jerusalem

When he was thirty-seven, he became king of all Israel and reigned for thirty-three years from Jerusalem. He was king for a total of forty years (2 Sam. 5:4–5 and 1 Chron. 29:27–28).

46–50: Bathsheba

The Bathsheba incident most likely occurred sometime between 46 and 50, after his commanders relegated him to the palace.

58–60: Absalom

The Absalom rebellion happened when David was around fifty-eight to sixty years old. Absalom had time to grow into adulthood. He was David's third son and was born after David became king in Hebron.

69: David anointed Solomon King

Solomon, David's second son with Bathsheba, was most likely about twenty or twenty-one years old when he became king upon David's death. He took charge in a mature way.

70: David's death

David died at age seventy, having enjoyed long life, wealth and honor.

BIBLIOGRAPHY

Binz, Stephen J. *David: Shepherd, and King of Israel*. Grand Rapids, Michigan: Brazos Press, 2011.

Floria, Cam. *David, A Man After God's Own Heart*. Lyrics to "The Lord Is My Shepherd," Ventura, California: Christian Artists Records, 1996.

Hillis, Newell Dwight. *David, the Poet and King*. Chicago, New York, Toronto: Fleming H. Revell Company, 1901.

Keller, W. Phillip. *A Shepherd Looks at Psalm 23*. Grand Rapids, Michigan: Zondervan, 1970.

Keller, W. Phillip. *David, the Shepherd King*. England: Word (UK) Ltd., 1986.

Keller, W. Phillip. *David, the Time of Saul's Tyranny*. England: Word (UK) Ltd., 1985.

Lawrence, Brother. *Practice the Presence of God*, Collected teachings by Brother Lawrence, compiled by Father Joseph de Beaufort.

Phillips, John. *Exploring the Psalms*. Volume One, Psalms 1-88. Neptune, New Jersey: Loizeraux Brothers, 1988.

Phillips, John. *Exploring the Psalms*. Volume Two, Psalms 89–150. Neptune, New Jersey: Loizeraux Brothers, 1988.

Wilkinson, Bruce, "The Prayer of Jabez." Colorado Springs, Colorado: Ovation Foundation, Inc., 2000.

LIVING THE CHRISTIAN LIFE IN TODAY'S WORLD BIBLE STUDY

Facilitator Guide and Ideas

THIS STUDY GUIDE is intended for either an individual or a group. It coincides with the chapters in this book to support the reader's commitment to become a person after God's heart. It reviews the story and the critical scriptures from each chapter and presents questions and discussion. Here are instructions for the facilitator to follow:

1. As the facilitator, create the right atmosphere and conditions in the meeting room or venue. Ask everyone to block out all other thoughts and focus on God's Word that will be read. Ask them to remove any obstacles and to do their best to grasp the meaning as it relates to them. Then review the story and comments. You or selected readers should read the scriptures out loud.

2. The questions and discussion to follow will seek to bridge the gap between the scripture itself and the Christian life today, as each person reflects on how these scriptures have meaning and come alive in their own lives. Guide the discussion, ask the questions, and respond to the answers, allowing participants the freedom to add their ideas and thoughts.

3. Following this, a time of prayer is important. It enables the participants to respond to the Word of God that has been read and discussed. There are many options for how to handle this, and it can be decided weekly.

4. After a time of talking to the Lord, a time of meditation or contemplation is suggested. This is a quiet time to let God speak to each person individually and to let the scriptures and prayers allow for a deeper awareness of God's presence in their lives.

5. Give participants an opportunity to talk about how they plan to live out the challenge from the Word of God that was read and discussed and the chapter that was reviewed. The purpose of this step is to hear how they plan to make action changes and how they plan to live and act in the coming week.

6. Conclude with prayer.

These thoughts and discussion ideas are based on Stephen J. Binz's "Ancient-Future Bible Study" method, which brings people together for a personal encounter with God through scripture, as taught in his many books.

Prelude: The Heart of the Matter

Please focus now on our discussion and the review of these scriptures. Let the past day and week fade away as we align our hearts in agreement.

This chapter reminds us that our "heart" is our inmost being, as David discussed in Psalm 103:1 and again in 139:23. Read these two scriptures. From here, in our hearts, we praise and worship the Lord. It is here that He looks to see who we really are and how we really are doing. He knows the real truth about us.

Remember now what He told Samuel in the very beginning when Samuel was looking over Jesse's sons. In 1 Samuel 16:7, the last part of the verse, God said, "The Lord does not look at the things man looks at. Man looks at the outward appearance, but the Lord looks at the heart."

Ask yourself this question: "What outward things do I look at, and what judgements do I make without knowing a person's heart?" Is this right, and is it fair?

Read Jeremiah 17:10: "I, the Lord, search the heart and examine the mind, to reward a man according to his conduct." What do you think God would find right now if He examined your heart?

What was found in David's heart is what we are considering in this book. David's words, from his life's lessons, to his son just after his anointing as the new king, are important for all of us. Read 1 Chronicles 28:9–10. Here are the important discussion points:

+ Wholehearted devotion

+ Having a willing mind

+ Motives behind thoughts and ideas

Read John 15:16. Jesus chooses, too! It implies that He has chosen you. How does that make you feel?

Our key verse from this chapter is from 2 Chronicles 16:9: "For the eyes of the Lord range throughout the earth to strengthen those whose hearts are fully committed to Him."

Are there some other scriptures that talk about commitment that you would like to read?

Do you want a committed heart for God? Pray out loud, individually, one at a time, this one simple sentence: "Lord, give me a committed heart for you."

Meditate on these scriptures we have discussed. Be quiet within yourself for a few moments, and listen for the Lord to speak to you.

How will these scriptures and your willingness to have a committed heart affect how you will feel and act this week?

Close in prayer.

One... Bring on the Giants

DAVID'S SECRET #1
He Did What God Wanted Him to Do

If your mind is full of today's activities, the things done and undone, do your best right now to let that go for a little while. Focus your heart and mind on these scriptures and the review of this chapter. We will be discussing God's will for your life.

The basic reason God chose David to be the next king, replacing Saul, was David's willingness to do whatever God asked him to do. Finding out what you believe God's will is for your life, and acting on it in a positive way, is the beginning of becoming a person after God's heart. It is His first requirement. It seems that even David, who God said would do whatever He wanted him to do, was often searching for what God's will was, as though he didn't really know.

In Psalm 143:8, 10, and 12, David is searching. Read it. It was the same in Psalm 40:8. When you read that again, think about your own desires. The secret of finding God's will is to genuinely desire it and pray that God will open your mind and heart to receive His answers.

In Psalm 25:4–5, David asks God to teach him. How might unplanned events in your life be explained as God teaching you about His will for your life?

The big question today is this: Do you desire to make a difference in this world? If you knew for sure that you could do that, would you be willing to take the consequences, both the easy ones and perhaps the difficult ones, to achieve it?

It would certainly expand your territory, your world of influence, and allow you a bigger ministry if your answer were yes.

How might desiring to do God's will all the time change your life?

Next, describe how you think God chooses people to do significant things for His Kingdom.

Let these scriptures and thoughts sink into your mind and heart. Take time right now to pray about these things. When you talk to the Lord, ask Him to show you His will and make you a more receptive Christian. Pray something like this out loud: "Dear Lord, please show me Your perfect will for my life, and open my heart to receive it."

After this time of prayer, be quiet, be still for a little while, and let God speak to your heart. Be receptive.

Make a list of the giants you might have to face this next week. How might wanting to do whatever God asks you to do impact your actions as you deal with these challenges?

Close in prayer, and ask for guidance and strength.

Two... Sit at God's Round Table

DAVID'S SECRET #2
He Was a Man of Integrity and Virtue

Talking about integrity and virtue is an extremely personal discussion. It comes home to each of us as we come face to face with how we act and our reasons for doing so. Concentrate now, and do your best to remove your fears of being honest with yourself and others. Clear your mind of roadblocks to the truth.

It is clear that God expects His followers to be above reproach. People value and trust someone who displays fairness and the virtues found in this chapter in their daily lives. None of us is perfect, but at some point we must realize and face any deficiencies we have and work hard to replace them with positive virtues.

List the ten virtues found in David's life. Do you see perseverance as one of your virtues, or do obstacles tend to stop you in your tracks? You are going to need perseverance to sit at God's round table!

In Psalm 26:2–3, David asked God to test and examine him. Read the text. At this point in his life, this boldness was part of who he was. Being truthful all the time would give us the same courage. He sounds the same in Psalm 7:8.

In Proverbs 3:3–4, God lets us know how He feels about boastful, proud attitudes. Read it again. Are you comfortable being around a boastful person? Honest humility is a true delight!

Many scriptures teach us how God looks at virtues and integrity. What other virtue-related scriptures are important to you? Read them out loud right now.

Patience is a virtue, so everyone says. Are you patient in waiting for God to answer your many requests? David waited at least twenty years to become the King of Israel, as God promised through Samuel when he was a teenager. It was a long wait, yet he never wavered in his belief. How strong is your belief? Are you willing to wait without losing trust?

Have you considered your loyalty to Jesus Christ? How deep is it? Who in your life are you most loyal to?

Knowing how God feels about generosity and giving with the right attitude and heart, how do you feel about tithing and giving gifts above and beyond? Do you think people look at you as a giver or a taker?

Knowing that God loves integrity, which of these virtues do you wish to imitate? Which ones do you see as weak spots in your life? Do you have any grey areas? How will you go about making the necessary changes?

Take a few minutes right now to pray that God will give you the desire to become a person with more integrity. If you have the time, ask the Lord about each of these ten virtues. As you embrace each one, you will become a positive light to others as they look at your life and how you live. Quietly let God speak to your heart. Listen....

What positive changes can you begin to make this next week as you learn to sit at God's round table?

Close in prayer, and pray for each other.

Three... Live in the Moment

DAVID'S SECRET #3
He Was a Man of Prayer

Close your eyes right now. We are going to talk about prayer, so blocking everything out you can see for a few moments will help you give your full attention to the scriptures we are about to read. We are going to consider the amazing opportunity we have to actually communicate with the Creator of the universe and explore how to listen to Him communicate back to us.

When David first arrived at Saul's court, he had a positive welcome and enjoyed favor with the king. But after his winning exploits against the Philistines, he became too popular and a threat to the king. He was facing antagonism from Saul's entire court. David couldn't understand it and told God about it all the time.

That's what was going on in Psalm 109. Read the first four verses. These kinds of difficulties helped mold him into becoming a man of prayer. Do you relate?

Read Psalm 5:3. Here, David talks about starting out his day with prayer. When is your prime time to pray? Notice the last part of the verse. David was expecting an answer! Do you think God responds positively when we have the faith to believe we will get an answer? Read James 1:6–8.

Jesus said He would give us whatever we asked for in His name. Read John 16:23–24 and Matthew 21:22. He promises us that we will have the answers and talks about our complete joy.... How great is that!

Jesus also talked about not using our prayers to promote our spirituality in Matthew 6:6 and 8. And James, his brother, said in his epistle, James 4:3, that you might not get an answer if you have wrong motives.... Read both of these scriptures out loud.

Praying out loud with a small group of people you don't know can be inhibiting. Consider letting prayer come spontaneously rather than going around the circle, especially in the beginning. Discuss this.

Read 1 Thessalonians 5:16–18. Verse 17 says to "pray continually," and the King James version says, "Pray without ceasing." Living today, with so many distractions in real life, this seems unrealistic. What do you think? If we learn to "practice the presence of God" in our consciousness, then talking to God is only a thought away at any time. That's why this chapter is titled "Live in the Moment."

Did you receive a direct answer to prayer recently, or even this year? What is the most outrageous thing you have ever prayed for?

Read Psalm 23. David looks at God as his shepherd. He talks about God taking care of all his physical and spiritual needs and protecting and comforting him in difficult situations. For David, God's blessing was all so positive that he ended with the belief that he has a destiny to fulfill.

In your prayer time right now, talk to God as your shepherd, and then take time to listen for the Lord's voice to speak to you as your shepherd. Close out the room now.... Listen. See His words.

How will you go about making changes in your prayer life this week?

Consider practicing the presence of God throughout each day, and try to emulate the qualities of a shepherd in your leadership responsibilities with work, family, and friends.

Four... Take the Heat

David's Secret #4

He was a Man of Repentance and Forgiveness

We need to put all other thoughts out of our minds except the word "forgive" and all its other forms: "forgiven," "forgiveness," and perhaps "confession" and even "repentance." Without them, we are lost. Take a look at those around you. All of them are forgiven. Close your eyes; see the forgiven faces. Clear your mind of anything else so we can explore the scriptures that have freed us.

We must understand that forgiveness is something everyone needs! Let's read Psalm 53:2–3, as well as Romans 3:11–12, quoting David's psalm and then our necessary response of faith in Christ by believing and receiving freely His grace, all found in Romans 3:21–24. After you have read these fabulous scriptures, thank the Lord out loud.

John, one of Jesus' closest disciples, said it powerfully in his letter in 1 John 1:9. Confession is difficult. Are you willing to take the heat and 'fess up? Some have said it is good for the soul, and it most certainly is. But the scripture goes further and says it is a requirement. What do you think? The other part is to receive and then believe. The same John said it in a straightforward way in John 1:12. These verses are the basis of our salvation. Is this what you believe as well?

After confessing his guilt, thinking he was going to die and instead receiving forgiveness, David felt such great relief. He talks about the forgiveness he felt in grand style in Psalm 103:1–5 and 10–12. Wow! How does that make you feel? God does not remember your sins once you have received His forgiveness. Can you do the same for someone who has wronged you? Jesus said how He feels about that in Luke 6:37 and 11:14. Read these two serious scriptures. Is there someone you need to forgive for whatever reason? Can you talk about it?

What about you? Are there are some situations you have never confessed and would like to be forgiven for? *Do it quietly right now.* He really is faithful and just to forgive you. Read Psalm 86:5.

David covered up his sin for a long time. The results were devastating, and he wrote about it in Psalm 32:1–5. How can repentance and forgiveness bring healing to an anxious and troubled heart?

Be quiet for a few minutes and think deep in your own heart. Can you remember some things God has forgiven you for that no one else even knows about? Thank Him over and over for cleansing you.

It is a beautiful thing, yet disturbing for some, that God often works through flawed people. Many believe it is the reason David's story is so powerful; it shows the depth and breadth of God's forgiveness and willingness to create a pure heart and a new creation out of sin and wrongful behavior.

Take time to pray now, and thank God for His unconditional forgiveness.

Feel His forgiveness for you personally. Listen for it within your heart.

Put forgiveness at the top of your list this week.

Seek out those you may have offended, and forgive anyone who dares to wrong you!

Close in prayer.

Five...All

He Loved God with All His Heart and All His Strength

Attention! Give this *all* of your focus and heart. When you read the word "greatest" a number of times in the scripture, from different sources, it really means something that is number one. These words are the greatest and most important words you will hear or read. Concentrate.

Read Deuteronomy 5:4, Matthew 22:37, and Mark 12:30. It is easy to see what these scriptures have in common. God wants our love. Throughout scripture, we are warned not to have other idols, which is anything that is more important to us than our love for the Lord. List some things that could easily be an idol in your life today.

Because heart and mind are both part of our innermost being, the strength part of God's commandment is what helps prove the "all" part of our requirement. The Bible is very clear that we are to work at it with all our heart and strength. Read Colossians 3:17 and 23. James also talked about proving our faith by working at it. Read James 2:18 and 19. We also have to be careful to understand that we are not earning our salvation. That is a free gift of grace and is not about works. As a reminder, read Ephesians 3:6–10, which talks about works in both ways.

"All" is a small but powerful word. Do you think it really means we are to love God with all our heart? What does "all" mean spiritually in your Christian life today?

How do you think God feels about a partial commitment? Read Revelation 3:15–16 and 20. David loved God so much that he wanted to build a great temple for His Name and His Glory.

But because David lived a life filled with warring and killing, God chose a man of peace, his son Solomon, to build the temple. David could have been disappointed, but instead he decided to give all his personal treasure so that he could be involved in being part of building the temple.

Are there some unfilled desires you have in your Christian life? How are you dealing with these unfulfilled dreams?

Because David just wanted to build God a house, God promised him a house and kingdom that would never end. As an extra, God added, "Now I will make your name great, like the names of the greatest men of the earth." The promise culminated in the birth and the life of Jesus Christ, a descendent of David. How does that make you feel about your attitude and God's promises?

David was constantly telling the Lord how much he loved Him. See Psalm 18:1, 86:12, 16:2, and 103:1. We often sing about God's love as well. What love songs to the Lord are your favorites? Sing one right now?

Pray out loud, answering this question: "I love you, Lord, because...."

Quietly, within yourself, contemplate your love for the Lord and His love for you. Listen for His promises to you.

How many people will you tell this week that you love the Lord? Bring the results the next time you are together!

Close in prayer.

Six... Be There, Like a Good Neighbor

DAVID'S SECRET #6

He Loved His Neighbors, His Family, and His Friends

Jesus talked about loving your neighbor as yourself almost like it was attached to "Love God with all your heart and strength." He placed high importance and value on it because it is something God requires of His followers. This seems more difficult living as a Christian today, not only because of our diverse world with all its variances and cultures, but also because we have neighbors who could be at odds with our beliefs and lifestyle in a hundred different ways.

Focus all your attention on these scriptures as we delve into this subject right now.

Read Romans 12:10. This verse that talks about honoring one another helps us understand what God and Jesus meant in Leviticus 19:18 and Matthew 22:39. In what practical ways can you honor someone above yourself? Do you think those scriptures really mean you have to love other people more than you love yourself?

Jesus brought it a little closer in Luke 6:31. How does it make you feel when a friend or neighbor does the opposite of that scripture?

David brought Jonathan's crippled son into his court and treated him like his own son after he was king. Why would David do that when the tradition was to eliminate all threats from the previous king's line?

Remembering how much David loved his own son, Absalom, do you think he felt responsibility for Absalom's death?

In Psalm 133:1–2, David describes how it feels to live in unity. However, if you have a real cantankerous neighbor or (friend), isn't it great to also read Romans 12:18? Even then, do you feel that you are the one required to live in peace? How does that work with Romans 12:3?

In today's world, what could be the result of your just being there and available for a neighbor? Read 2 Timothy 2:24–25.

Make a list of people in your life who are easy to love. Then make a list of those who are a challenge. What does "Love them by faith" mean?

Pray for some of the people on your list. Also pray for each other, that God will give each of you a heart of love for your neighbors.

As you sit quietly, let the Lord speak to your heart about how to love your neighbors as yourself. Look at the scriptures just discussed. Think about unity and honoring a friend or family member or another Christian. Now let God place some names and faces before you. Pray for them, and listen to what the Lord is asking you to do about it.

Have you ever tailgated the back bumper of a slow driver to the point of their discomfort, and then, when you passed the car, you recognized the driver as someone you knew or even someone you see at church?

What real actions will you take this week to make sure your neighbors know there has been a change in you?

Think about memorizing Romans chapter 12.

Close in prayer.

Seven... Cry Out and Shout!

DAVID'S SECRET #7
He Had a Heart of Worship

Sing a few favorite worship songs as you begin your study today.

Having a heart of worship also means having a heart of gratitude and expressing thankfulness melded with adoration and praise for the Lord God. These expressions can be said out loud with shouts of joy or stated quietly with introspection deep in your heart.

Now consider the power and importance of the scriptures you are about to read, giving them your total, worshipful focus and attention.

Read Psalm 29:2. David did this all the time. In Psalm 9:1–2, he explains what his feelings are and what his response is when he gives this kind of Glory to the Lord by praising Him with all his heart. It results in his telling others, being glad, rejoicing, and singing praise to His Name.

When you praise His name, what and how does it make you feel?

When is your favorite, prime time to worship the Lord? Do you prefer worshipping quietly within your heart or loudly with a group? Do you ever raise your hands? Do you clap your hands at Sunday worship and dance back and forth with the music? Do the instruments enhance your Sunday worship experience?

We read that when David brought the ark of God back to Jerusalem, he did it while dancing and singing. Psalm 68:24–26 tells the story. Wouldn't you have loved to be in the crowd for one of David's praise events? Can you imagine four thousand instrumentalists and unnumbered singers? At the end of the instructions for the building of the temple and the anointing of Solomon, David praised the Lord in front of the whole assembly in 1 Chronicles 29:10–13. Then they celebrated in verses 21 and 22. List some ways you could become less fearful and inhibited in your worship experience.

Two of David's psalms have a similar theme. The passage in Psalm 96:9–13 is off-the-charts exciting, and Psalm 19:1–4 explains what it really means and what is happening. But Jesus, in Luke 19:39–40, goes even further, saying it could have been a literal happening! How does that make you feel? Can you sing the world's most popular song, "How Great Thou Art," without looking at the lyrics?

David had a private worship side, too. He worshipped privately in Psalm 40:1–3, and the result of his new commitment was that people would put their trust in the Lord. This could be a fulfillment of your calling as well. However, do you think that people sometimes use God's favor or a worship experience for personal or political advantage?

Jesus also mentioned the kind of worshiper the Father seeks in John 4:23–24. Reread the lyrics to the song "Heart of Worship." Would you consider yourself a "true worshipper?"

Pray out loud beginning with the phrase, "Lord, give me a heart of worship today…." Then, at the end of your prayer time, sit quietly and worship the Lord. Listen for His love song to you.

Make a plan to worship the Lord this week in ways and places other than at church. What are some good possibilities?

Close in prayer.

Eight... You Can Do This

"DAVID'S SEVEN SECRETS"
He Was a Man After God's Own Heart

Use the six pages of "Become a Person After God's Own Heart" as your study guide for this week. If this is your desire, then open your heart and let these scriptures and ideas soak in.

Read Philippians 3:10–14, and discuss the idea of having to work on becoming a person after God's heart because you have not arrived yet.

Read Romans 12:1–2. Did you realize that this is a way to be able to test and approve what God's will is for your life?

Why do you think God created man? Read 1 Chronicles 29:17, Genesis 1:27–28, and Revelation 15:2–4. Did God create us to worship Him?

Are you really ready to "press on to reach the goal of becoming a person after God's heart"? Say it out loud to those you are with: "I am ready to press on to become a person after God's heart."

Read each of the seven steps one at a time. Read the scriptures and discuss what your response and actions will be after each one.

When you have finished, pray that each person will achieve his or her goal.

Quietly meditate on what that really means to you, and then listen for the Holy Spirit to tell you that He will be there with you to help you achieve the goal and to give you the desire of your heart.

What is the first thing you will do this week to start your journey to become a person after God's heart?

After these testimonies, close in prayer.

Read each of the seven steps from time to time along with the scriptures and consider what your response and actions will be after each one. Press on...

ACKNOWLEDGMENTS

FIRST AND MOST importantly to Danette Ferro, a real friend for over 50 years, who painstakingly edited every word I wrote in this book.

She offered her excitement and joy when she loved something and had great ideas when it came time to consider changes and re-writes. In this way she was very gentle with a first-time author from 2,000 miles away. Thanks as well to her husband, Bob Ferro, who gave up a lot of time with his wife for this project.

Thanks to my daughter Ballad Sweeney and her husband Mike, and children Owen and Liam for taking such good care of me as I recovered from a couple of Achilles surgeries and used their home as my base to write and re-write much of this book as I healed up over two three-month periods. And thanks to daughter Regan McCraley who brought me lunch from time to time.

Thanks to good friends Jim and Karen Schmidt, Monty and Christa Kelso, Julia and Bob Hamilton, Liz Selleck, Joe Huntsman, Lori Stern, Holly Potter, Byron Spradlin, Cher Nelson, Thurlow Spurr and Jon and Mimi Stemkoski who gave their time and encouragement along the way.

I want to give special appreciation to Rev. Denny and Leesa Bellesi. Denny was the first pastor to recognize the value of this book and it was his initial response that really helped me believe even stronger in the message of this project. I also want to thank my own pastor, Rev. Bob Hallman who gave me a big push in the very beginning as well as Rev. Glenn Gunderson and Rev. Dave Booye who were wonderfully encouraging. It was these church leaders that saw the need and provided the vision for the Bible Study at the end of this book, "Living the Christian Life in Today's World." My prayer is that it will help their respective church families to grow, as many of them work at becoming people after God's heart.

A big thanks to Liza Mena, my production and final edit person at Higher Life, and, of course, David Welday for his ideas and edits, and the rest of his dedicated staff at Higher Life Publishing for sticking with me through all the changes and additions!

Discover
The
Seven
Secrets
of Becoming a
Person
After God's
Own Heart

CONTINUE THE CONVERSATION

If you believe in the message of this book and would like to share in the ministry of getting this important message out, please consider taking part by:

- Writing about *David's 7 Secrets* on your blog, Twitter, Instagram and Facebook page.

- Suggesting *David's 7 Secrets* to friends and send them to the author's website www.continentalsglobalfoundation.org

- When you're in a bookstore, ask them if they carry the book. The book is available through all major distributors, so any bookstore that does not have it in stock can easily order it.

- Encourage your book club to read *David's 7 Secrets*.

- Writing a positive review on www.amazon.com

- Purchase additional copies to give away as gifts.

Sing with Thurlow Spurr's

VIRTUAL CHOIR
Without leaving home...

For Information:

www.americayourebeautiful.com

877.877.6010

CAM FLORIA IS available for speaking engagements at your event. If you would like to invite him as a guest speaker for part, or all, of a series on "Becoming a Person After God's Own Heart," or Bible Study discussions on *David's 7 Secrets*, please contact our associates through the email below to schedule him and for more information. As Mr. Floria lives in Hawaii, advanced notice is always helpful.

TOPICS of interest:

+ Author of *David's 7 Secrets*

+ Founder of the Continental Singers, currently 25 international groups

+ Executive Producer of Christian Artists' Seminar in the Rockies, 1975 through 2000

+ Written nine musicals, including "David A Man After God's Own Heart," and the Dove Award winner, "Dreamer"

+ Produced over 70 recording projects domestically and over 50 international projects using his recorded tracks and vocal arrangements

+ Created scripts and programs for all traveling groups

+ Leadership Workshops for all Directors of Continental Singers groups

Please contact him through:
info@christianartistsbooks.com
To purchase additional copies

A Man
After
God's Own
Heart

What kind of a man?